Cherish – A Memoir

The Truth About Where I Came From and Who I Loved

Tony Albano

PARK PLACE PUBLICATIONS
Pacific Grove, California

Copyright © 2021 Anthony Albano
ISBN 978-1-953120-34-2
First Edition June 2021

Front cover photo: Tony in front of The Other End on Bleeker Street in Greenwich Village, 1973.
Photo taken by Big Ed.
Back cover photo: Tony on the Monterey Penunsula with his three-legged companion. Brie.
All other photos from the author's personal archives.

Park Place Publications
Pacific Grove, California
parkplacepublications.com

Dedication

*This book could only be dedicated
to my wife, Pat, who has waited forty
years for me to tell this story.*

*And to the people who still
have the spirit of 1969.*

Acknowledgments

In the process of writing this book, I have learned that it takes a village. I would like to thank:

My test readers—Chuck Goldberg, Andy Kesler, Lois Mayol, Jaimie Passmore, JoAnn Reiter, Nancy Rexford, Carol Seril, and Lavada Watson for their time, support, and feedback.

Alison Kaufman Rease for typing the earliest version of this book.

Margie McCurry, a true believer from the beginning, who on that wonderful afternoon at Duffy's, guided me toward performing as a storyteller and recording and publishing my stories in print. She said that since I could not afford her as a publicist, she would be mine for free and then tirelessly promoted my endeavors and my work in every way she could. She also patiently read through different versions of my book and provided her expert feedback. Without her encouragement and belief in me, I never would have gotten to this point in my life.

Nina Solomita, my editor, who utilized her top-notch skills to clarify and organize the content, all the while staying true to my authentic voice. Early on, vi

my wife Pat announced that Nina was the boss, and that I should listen to her! When I got lazy and just wanted to ad lib, she pushed me to write out the text on paper. When I got discouraged, she used humor to re-energize me. And Nina was the only one I finally felt at ease enough with to communicate the more intimate moments of my story. Along the way we became such good friends that now I tell her she's stuck with me. I also want to take this opportunity to apologize to her for driving her crazy. It is not an exaggeration to say that I could never have completed this book without her.

Many people advised me that I should send the manuscript to traditional publishing houses. But being 65 years old, I didn't feel that I had the time, so I went back to Patricia Hamilton at Park Place Publications, who did a great job publishing my second book, *A Leg to Stand On*. For a story this important to me, I wanted a reliable and creative person that I could trust.

Prologue

I am a storyteller and a keeper of memories. I tell stories to help others notice and appreciate the magical moments of their lives, ones they may have forgotten or may not think were significant. Until the last couple of years, I have performed my stories orally to groups. I do not consider myself a writer, so no one is more surprised than I am to have two books out of short stories of my own experiences. And, of course, those stories being about life, include events that stir the emotions from happiness to grief and all those in between. It is so rewarding to get emails from my readers telling me that my stories brought up similar memories for them.

This book, however, is quite different from the first two. It is a memoir describing my life from birth to the age of eighteen, the years that shaped who I am today. It contains stories I have never told to an audience but only to the people closest to me and some not even to them. For many years I was ashamed of where I came from, my upbringing and my family. Now, with the passing of time and, hopefully, having gained some maturity and wisdom, I have learned to appreciate, love, and hold close the colorful characters that made up my early life—their struggles and contradictions, their joys and celebrations, their street wisdom and unique moral codes in addition to their sometimes-questionable relationship with the law, and above all, their passion for baseball and love for animals. I now recognize that, not only do I have nothing to be ashamed of but much to be proud of. I am aware that my early experiences were probably more full of adventure and excitement than many kids who had traditional, comfortable upbringings. I had a secret life with my grandfather, who I called Gramps. He not only loved me, but shared escapades usually hidden from children my age, and I loved every minute of it.

The most important lesson I learned from my gramps was *to believe* that anything was possible if you believed hard enough. This has held true all my life. One of my earliest passions bore this out when I focused my energy and belief into a new and pretty terrible baseball team—the New York Mets. From the time they started out they were considered the worst professional baseball team to ever take the field. But I believed that someday they would walk in the sun, and I was willing to wait.

As the Mets matured and came into their own, so did I. As a kid, I loved coin collecting, animals, music, and, above all, my Mets. There was one more love. When I was fourteen, I began a second secret life—an unconventional, one might say shocking, relationship.

Although some would question the morality of such a connection, the truth is that the experience was beautiful and life-changing, and I wouldn't trade it for the world. The song from that time that most captures this kind of love is "Cherish." I truly cherish what happened. This story is one I have kept secret for fifty years. It is time to tell it.

Please note that there are words and phrases I used that were the language of the era that are no longer appropriate now, but I wanted to capture the times and neighborhoods I grew up in. I hope that my writing skills did justice to this beautiful story. All I ask is for you to please read it with an open mind.

Everything here is true, but one person's name has been changed to preserve her privacy.

Table of Contents

Cherish – A Memoir

The Truth About Where I Came From and Who I Loved

My Back Pages

"She's a whore." My first memory is of my mother screaming those words at my grandfather. For as long as I can remember, as far back as I can, I always end up with the same event. It's at the apartment on Howard Avenue in Brooklyn, the second place that we lived, but the first I can recall. It's like I'm watching a play. My grandfather is sitting at the kitchen table. I'm about three or four years old, and I'm holding onto his leg while my mother yells and waves a finger in his face. "She's a whore and she'll always be a whore, and, as far as I'm concerned, she's nothing to me. She's dead!"

My grandfather pleads with her. "Mary, please stop! Don't say those things, especially in front of Anthony. He shouldn't hear you speak like this about your mother. You don't know the whole story. You're wrong about her. She's still your mother."

"I'll spit on her grave!"

I didn't know what whore meant or what was really going on, but my four-year-old mind told me that it couldn't be good. To see my grandfather, who I called Gramps, being so tormented really hurt. The only thing I could do was stay by his side and hug him and put my head on his big belly. I knew that when my mother got like that, it was best not to say anything back because it would only prolong her ranting. Unfortunately for Gramps, he would try again to explain himself, but you couldn't win with her.

"Mary," he would say, "It wasn't your mother's fault. It was me. I was a terrible husband; I'd go out with the guys and drink and not come home when I should have been home with you and your sister. Your mother just got fed up with me."

This made things worse, my mother more furious. I could just feel the explosion coming; it was the regular routine. She was on fire and there was no stopping her. Leaning over him, she would back him up into his chair, and say, "As far as I'm concerned, I don't have a mother! She died the day she left me and my sister, and I don't care if you were a terrible husband and a drunk. If you were no good, fine! She should have left you. I don't blame her for that, but you still take your kids. I mean, a dog takes better care of her puppies, better than that tramp. She's lower than a dog. So, don't tell me that's my mother and I should have some respect. I curse the day that bitch left me and my sister behind."

My grandfather was leveled and embarrassed that I had to hear all this. He could never win the war of words with her, for she was the best, the champ, at unleashing the most potent poison that would devastate even the toughest person. But he never stopped trying.

With the final blow, all was quiet except for Gramps whispering in my ear. As I clung to him, he would say, "Anthony, don't pay attention to her. She doesn't mean what she says. She's just bitter and mad at the world. Believe me, Anthony, your grandmother was a good woman. It was me. Don't be stupid and make the same mistakes I did." He spoke to me as if I were an adult. I remember this so vividly; the warning about not making his mistakes would become his mantra for the rest of our lives together. He would say it every time he felt bad about the past that haunted him.

After that, the apartment was still. To keep the peace, the three of us retreated into our own little worlds. As time went on and these outbursts continued to occur, I learned that often, amazingly, within a couple of hours something would break the ice, like my father would come home from work in a good mood ready to tell us the story of his day or put a record on the hi fi and start singing to my mother. And Gramps and I would crack up watching my mother pushing him away, saying he was crazy, but loving it. He'd sing songs like, You Made Me Love You, I Didn't Want To Do It. Gramps and I would be having so much fun; we'd egg him on to keep it going. My father was usually a quiet man but loved having an audience, and once he heard our approval, he'd go all out. He would drop down to one knee with his arms stretched out Al Jolson-style and sing to my mother. Then she'd accuse him of drinking, and he would say things like, "Mary, it's just love."

It was wild. It couldn't get any better than this! They were having so much fun. Just when life got really low, we always got what we needed most. Suddenly the horrible fighting and yelling earlier became nothing but a passing storm. Nothing could equal the pleasure and security Gramps and I got from seeing my mother and father happy and having a good time. We wished it could always be like that. I know that's not realistic, but Gramps and I were not realistic. We wanted the fun to last forever.

I'll Be Home for Christmas

My mother never got over the fact that her mother left her and her sister Jeanette behind when she went off with a sailor on leave. The story goes that it was 1943, and Theresa, her mother, and Theresa's sister, Sonia, met two sailors at Nedick's Hotdog Stand in Coney Island. These two married sisters, who both had children, forgot everything but their own pleasures, and as their flings continued, they came up with a plan. My grandmother told her husband Jimmy that she needed a little rest from the kids, and that she was going to visit one of her sisters for four or five days. She assured him and her two daughters, Mary, five, and Jeanette, two, that she would be home for Christmas. Theresa and Sonia had no intentions of coming back. They were off and running, starting new lives with these men. Christmas came and went without any sign of my grandmother.

After that, my distraught grandfather had a shattering nervous breakdown. Besides being unable to take care of his two daughters, he was unable to take care of himself. His family, realizing what bad shape he was in, did the best they could. My mother was sent to live with my grandfather's brother, her Uncle Johnny and his wife, Marie, who had three daughters and a son. My Aunt Jeanette was sent to live with Aunt Gracie, my grandfather's sister. My grandfather was left to drink himself into oblivion then sleep wherever he flopped. The world was a lot more innocent, and mothers leaving their children was unheard of back then, which made this episode more shocking to all those involved. The thing that infuriated my mother even more was that her mother's sister did eventually return and took her children back when her own mother did not.

When Uncle Johnny took his five-year-old niece, Mary, to his home, he told his wife, Marie, "From now on, Mary lives with us, and that's that."

Marie was a kind, loving soul, a little dizzy. Uncle Johnny ruled the house like it was his castle. He was considered a tough guy and looked like a retired heavyweight boxer. I'd never seen thicker fingers than his; they looked like Italian sausages. Even though she had no say in the matter, Aunt Marie was glad to help. The two of them did the best they could trying to make my mother feel like one of their own, and life with them was adequate under the circumstances. My mother said she would always be grateful to her uncle and aunt because they stepped in and gave her a home. But no matter how nice they were, it was not the same.

If nothing else, my mother had one good thing on her side. She was blessed with good looks. She grew from a five-year-old child into a striking teenager—an Elizabeth Taylor-look- alike. The resemblance was remarkable. Aunt Marie saw trouble on the way as the boys and older men were taking notice of her niece. Being separated from her sister Jeanette led my mother to have more than the normal teenage rebellion. When Aunt Marie got wind that one of the Albano brothers was after my mother, she had to step in with some motherly advice, telling her, "Whatever you do, please stay away from the Albanos. They're not good for marrying. They're nice people, but they're wild, good to have on your side as a friend, but they don't make good husbands."

The Albanos, nicknamed "the Mazzines," which meant coming from a tribe of people living by their own rules, had quite a reputation in the neighborhood. Ten brothers and one sister, with the father at the head. They were either loved or feared. Either way, when you heard the name Mazzine, you had an opinion. No one in the neighborhood, even the police, wanted to mess with them. Even Grandpa Mazzine's wife, Josey, was well-known for her untraditionally Italian style of motherhood. The more Aunt Marie harped about staying away from them, the more my mother went out of her way to find them. She ended up with my father, Pete, who at age twenty-six, was ten years older than her.

My father was always more responsible than his wayward brothers. As soon as he got my mother pregnant, he got a city job. This was hard to do because he had a criminal record, but in New York, people owed one another favors, and somebody owed his older friend, Sonny, a favor. Sonny got my father a job working for the highway department paving the streets. Though he loved his brothers and his brothers loved him, he was considered the straight one, a bit of a stiff. When he got his Elizabeth Taylor-look-alike girlfriend pregnant, he felt he had to do the right thing and marry her.

My newlywed parents, Mary and Pete Albano, didn't have any money so they had no choice but to have me delivered at the county hospital. The coming of the first child usually is a joyful event, but that wasn't the case for my mother, and she wasn't going to let me forget it.

"Anthony," she would say, "that King's County Hospital didn't care. Nobody cares when you don't have no money. I never saw the same doctor twice. I didn't know the doctor who delivered you. The day you were born I didn't get any rest because people I didn't know kept coming in and out of the room, strangers bringing in other poor girls like me. It was filthy dirty lying there. I watched the roaches crawling up the floorboards and paint peeling off the walls."

Then she would come to the grand finale—the words I hated most, ones that would haunt me for years and cut me the deepest. "Because of that hospital, I can't have no more children. Who the hell knows what they did to me up there? They ruined my insides. They didn't know what the hell they were doing. I went through some hell to have you! I sacrificed my life! I hope you appreciate what I went through to have you!"

When I was born, my parents lived in a run-down tenement that backed up against a brewing company. My mother told me that all night long you could hear the trucks loading for early morning deliveries. At dawn, all the truck drivers would start their engines so close to our building that it felt like you were in the truck. My mother was only seventeen when she gave birth to me in April, and, according to her, that summer of 1955 broke all records for being the hottest summer in decades. She told me that each day was more humid than the next. She said the smell of beer just hung in the air like a black cloud. She said she almost felt drunk, she was so hot. Also, she reminded me I had colic and was sickly, and I would not stop crying all day and all night until she would pick me up. She said she couldn't even go to the bathroom without me, and at times she thought she would crack; dark thoughts would come into her mind, and she thought of throwing me out the same window that the hot air was coming in just to get it over with. By the time she would come to the end of one of her tirades, even though I had heard this repertoire many times, I would still squirm inside, the guilt so powerful it made my legs wobble.

I have to say these outbursts didn't happen often as long as things were going her way. Most of the time she was fun, vulnerable, kind of naive. She was like a child in many ways, and as I got older, I felt like the adult.

I was always happy to have been born in April. In New York, after months of the cold winter, no matter how bad the past has been, this special time of year brings a fresh start. Most New Yorkers have no time for complaining or feeling sorry for themselves. They're too busy with the visions of good times ahead. They feel a renewed faith that things will get better, and they will walk in the sun. Ask any true believer and he'll tell you even the air smells different in April, not like any other time of the year. The scent of hope—it's pure magic! So, in April 1955, while Brooklyn was getting ready for the beginning of baseball season with their beloved Dodgers, my family was getting ready to have me. They tell me I was due on the 16th, but I kept them waiting until the 21st.

Gramps would always tell me that "God makes you wait for great things, so we appreciate them."

After we left the tenement where I spent my first years, we moved to 514 Howard Avenue. Among the few memories of Howard Avenue that stand out in my mind was when my father went crabbing in the summertime. I was so excited when he woke me up out of my sleep to show me a bathtub of live crabs. I was three or four and fascinated and stared at them for hours. My father told me, "Don't touch them. They bite. I'll show you how to handle them." At that point, the crab bit him, and he said, "I told you they bite."

Another thing I remember about my father that happened more than once while I was still young enough to be in a crib were the mornings I would hear the familiar snap snap of mouse traps going off. I would stay quiet in the crib in the dark until I heard my father say, "We got one, Mary! I think it's the one I set behind the refrigerator. They like it there because it's warm."

When I heard him, I knew I could make a move. I would stand up and hold onto the side bars of the crib and tell them I was scared. I really wasn't, but I knew this would get my father to take me out of the crib and let me sleep with them in the pull-out Castro convertible in the living room. Those were my favorite nights. I couldn't wait for the morning to come to see what our catch would bring us. As soon as my father woke up, he went straight to the traps. If we got two, my father was thrilled. Once we got three, and he acted like he had hit the daily number. He had his own style of getting rid of the unlucky ones that got caught. It was simple. He would bring the trap to the back window of the kitchen, lift the trap lever, and let the poor creature free fall from the fourth floor down to the back alley onto sparkling shattered glass and broken dreams below.

One day at the very moment that he was showing me his technique to release the mouse, a man on the second floor stuck his head out the window directly below us. As we watched it fall, it seemed like it was in slow motion. My father quickly grabbed me and pulled me away from the window so we would be out of sight.

Sure enough, it landed right on this man's head. We could hear him yelling, "I'll get you guys up there!"

My father was laughing so hard, he had to hold his stomach. He said, "Anthony! It's a good thing that guy had his cap on," like that would make it all okay.

My mother got a job when we lived at Howard Avenue, and Gramps would come watch me every day. Both my parents were happy that Gramps looked after me while they were at work, and he was thrilled. One day he taught me how to fill balloons with water and drop them off the fire escape on people below. His reasoning was that we were helping people cool off in the heat of the summer. When my father got home and learned of our activities, he was very upset with my grandfather, which was unusual. Apparently he didn't remember that he was the one who taught me to drop mice on people's heads.

Once my mother bought me a Dixie cup, half vanilla, half chocolate ice cream, and she told me I could sit on the stoop. Somehow or other, I found another kid, a black kid, to share the ice cream with. We shared it with the same wooden spoon. He ate the vanilla side, and I ate the chocolate side. At the age of four, I'd never learned about prejudice or who I was supposed to share with. Then my mother came down and saw us. She was very upset. She had always told me to share, and I did! And now she was furious. I didn't understand.

Even though she could be verbally mean, one of the few times my mother was physical with me was after she had just finished mopping the floor. She had given me a bowl of soup to eat and, after I ate it, I threw up on the clean floor. She got angry and took my face and smeared it into the vomit. She was screaming that I messed up her clean floor. If my grandfather had been there, he would have killed her.

My final memory of Howard Avenue is connected to the fact that my mother would not let my father name me Perry after his favorite singer, Perry Como. One day my father was late coming home from work. He finally arrived home all smiles; he held a little box in one hand, a bag in the other. He had brought home a beautiful golden, orange canary complete with a cage, accessories, and even a 45-vinyl record to teach the bird to sing. Our new addition already had a name— Perry. My father would talk to Perry for hours, trying to get him to sing. If my father wasn't at work, he was consumed with his canary. One day when my mother had enough of the "Pete and Perry show," she turned to me with only a look that she could give, and, in all seriousness, she said, "Anthony, your father is a nut! He loves that friggin' bird more than me. He thinks he's 'The Birdman of Alcatraz!'"

Sometimes, when it would get really hot in the apartment, my father would worry about Perry, so he would put him out on the fire escape to get him some fresh air. One afternoon he let out a yell of horror. We ran out to see what happened. My father was devastated, discovering he had left the cage open on the fire escape, and Perry was gone. He told us we had to leave the empty bird cage out there with the door open in case Perry would come home, and for the first couple of days, the first thing he would say when he came home from work was, "Is Perry back?"

Finally, my mother said, "Pete, get real. The bird is not coming back just like my mother. They just leave. They don't even say goodbye."

My Secret Life

Everyone called my gramps, whose name was James Maturo, "Juicy" because if he didn't have a Pall Mall in his mouth, he had a piece of Juicy Fruit gum, but, to me, he was just Gramps. Gramps had been through hell and back. He lost his leg when he was seventeen in an elevator accident. It was amputated because gangrene set in. If it happened today, he probably wouldn't have lost his leg. When my grandmother didn't come home that first Christmas as she had promised, his life spun out of control. He drank heavily and slept wherever he fell. Losing all sense of responsibility, he was on a one-man suicide mission. Alone, he continued his rampage, and one night, in a drunken stupor, he stepped out in front of a bus and was critically injured. They say he broke just about every bone in his body and was near death; the doctors said the only thing that kept him alive was his strong heart. That, he had—he had the biggest heart I've ever known.

After a long recuperation, he was awarded a fairly large sum of money from the City of New York. This gave him free rein for more drinking and reckless living. I heard that at one point, he used his award to buy some lots in New York that were valuable, but little by little he sold them off. He would throw his money around wastefully, helping his many so-called friends. When the money was gone, his so-called friends were gone too. He was in and out of mental institutions. They tried everything that medical science had to offer at the time—rest, group therapy, even shock treatments, but nothing seemed to work. Juicy had become a forgotten person in most people's lives until one special event occurred—my birth.

Somehow, some way, something clicked in his head and brought him back to life and behaving in normal way. People were baffled by the total mental change that he went through on becoming a grandfather. He stopped living in the past and stopped crying over his past sins and losses. He now had another chance and purpose for living. From what I've heard, from the moment I was brought home from the hospital, they couldn't keep him away. He was there morning, noon, and night. He got himself a rented room at a boarding house, quit drinking, and went on welfare because he was out of money. The person who would have angry outbursts at bars, urinate in his pants, flop wherever he was, and blame everyone for his problems was not the Gramps I had ever seen. Just as I was the right person for him at that time in his life, he was the right person for me at that time.

The family was still a little skeptical about the changes in Gramps, but as weeks turned into months and into years, everyone, including my parents, happily accepted the new Juicy. When he proved he was capable of taking care of me, they both realized that my mother could go to work to help bring more money into the house, and they had a built-in babysitter.

The Gramps I knew was not a depressed person. He walked with confidence and, in his care, I felt completely safe and carefree. Wherever we went together, and we were together a lot, we were welcomed as "Juicy and the Kid." This was the beginning of our secret life. I know we did things we were not supposed to do, saw things we were not supposed to see, but I loved every minute of it. I wouldn't have changed it for anything in the world.

My mother got a job in the hat department at Abraham and Straus Department Store, a classy New York store of the era. She reminded us over and over that not everyone could sell hats; you had to have a beautiful face for that. She knew she looked a lot like Elizabeth Taylor. With neither parent home, Gramps and I enjoyed endless time together. Until I could walk well enough to keep up with him, wooden leg and all, we would just spend time playing with my little soldiers, cowboys and Indians, my Fort Apache set, and sometimes we even got into mischief, throwing water balloons off the fire escape. I always knew how far we could go without getting into too much trouble because I never wanted anything to keep us from being together. My parents reminded him over and over not to spoil me. At some point, my grandfather started cooking dinner for us, and it would be ready for my father when he came home from work and for my mother before she went to work. He was so anxious to be involved with me that when my father said he liked pepper and eggs, my grandfather made it for him for four straight nights.

Finally, my father said, "Juicy, what's with the peppers and eggs?"

My grandfather said, "You said you liked it!"

"Yeah, but not every night!"

One of my treats in life was that my mother brought home a little toy for me every night after work. They cost less than a dollar, and I loved the surprise. I waited for her to come home with the toy and to see the latest style in hats.

Then the fun really began. When I was old enough, we could leave the house together, Gramps and me. Usually, we traveled by bus. He never drove because of his bad leg. Occasionally, we even took a cab. Every morning, after my father would go to work, Gramps would be there. I'd get dressed, and we'd be on our way. We traveled on our own route and did exciting things. During the day we'd go to Flatbush Avenue where all the shopping was and along the way we'd stop and have breakfast at a diner, then visit friends or relatives. We always had to stop at Jeffrey's Bakery to bring pastry home. Toward the end of our route, we went into a toy shop where I could pick out anything I wanted.

He would talk to the owner of the store while I had free rein. Even at that age I knew not to go overboard because he would have bought me anything, and I didn't want him to get in trouble.

Sometimes, we even stopped at my other grandparents' home, the Mazzine house, which was off limits as far as my mother was concerned; she didn't approve of their way of life. Of course, I would never say we went there. We were welcomed with friendly greetings; they loved Juicy and were happy to see their first grandson. There was another grandchild who was older than me. Her name was Joanne, but because she was a girl and didn't have the status a boy had and had the stigma of being a dwarf, she was never really appreciated or recognized as the first grandchild.

Wherever we went, Gramps and I were a hit. Looking back, I guess it was because my grandfather had almost been forgotten, and, at that time with me, he was strutting down the street like he was the mayor of the city, hair slicked back, cigarette hanging out of his mouth, dressed impeccably. I felt like he was a locomotive, and I was his caboose. Nothing ever got in our way, and I never had a trace of fear when I was with him. His swagger made me feel like we were invincible. He was a round man who reminded me of Jackie Gleason. When he entered a place, things happened.

My favorite place we went to eat was White Castle. We'd go in there and sit at the counter and he knew all the waitresses. He'd flirt with them and they would flirt back, saying, "Juicy, you've got the kid with you today!"

He would answer, "Of course, we're a team."

On the White Castle bag was written, "Eat them by the sack!" They were little square burgers, tasty, with onions on top, and boy, did I eat them by the sack.

Every once in a while, my parents would let me sleep at his boarding house in his room, but we really never slept there. He would take me to a girlfriend's house. Once, I remember the lady he visited had a boy a few years older than me. He was nice enough to share his toys and his bed with me. I knew, even at that age, to stay in the room with the kid and not ruin any fun my grandfather would be having in the other room.

Probably the most secretive thing we did together was to go to a neighborhood bar. When we walked in, Juicy's beer was put right in front of him and my Coke with a cherry was waiting for me and, boy, did I get the royal treatment from his friends. If there was a woman at the bar, and my grandfather was having a conversation with her, I knew to get lost for a while. It was okay with me because, while Gramps was making his move at the bar, the other customers would give me dimes to play the shuffleboard bowling game with the sawdust on it that I was finally tall enough to reach. While I was with Gramps, I never saw him overdrink, behavior far different from the stories I'd heard. When we were running late and he had to get home to make dinner, we took a cab. We had to really move.

First question my mother would ask when we got home: "Were you at a bar? I smell beer."

Gramps would say, "Mary, are you crazy? I'd never take Anthony to a bar!"

Then she'd ask me, "Anthony, did he take you to a bar?"

I'd say, "No, Mommy. Not at all."

Her favorite line was, "I can't win! One lies and the other one swears."

She would then threaten that if he were taking me to bars, she'd take me away from him. Gramps and I would exchange a look of conspiracy when she wasn't looking.

One day, my mother and I walked to a comer store and a big scene was going on across the street. Two men with no shirts on were having a knife fight. In the heat of the summer, people gathered around them in a circle. The crowd egged them on. My mother said to keep walking and not to look. So, of course, I looked. Right at that moment, one man sliced the other man's arm, and he must have hit an artery because the blood was spurting out like a geyser. The next second, four police cars arrived, and my mother rushed me back into the house.

She said, "Those Puerto Ricans, they love their knives."

When my father came home from work, she told him about what happened and said, "Petie, there was an incident outside today. Those Spics are at it again, and Anthony saw the whole thing."

I think this episode started the wheels turning in my father's head that it was time to get out of the neighborhood, especially because in a year or two I'd be going to school. My father, with only a grammar school education, was streetwise and had common sense. His older friend Sonny, my Uncle Frank, was a big influence on him in all good ways. He would tell my father, "Now that you are married and have a kid, you can't live the way your family does." Lucky for me, my father always listened to him. Uncle Frank was his mentor.

Right around the time we left Howard Avenue, there was a movie being made on the street. I guess they wanted to show what real life was like. So, of course, all the movie lights, the directors, and actors were right below our apartment. My father teased my mother and told her to come down with him.

"Mary, I'll get you into the movies because you have that beautiful face. Ya gotta have nerve in this world to get ahead," my father said. "They'll spot you and you'll be a star!"

She did go down, and Gramps and I watched from the fire escape. We thought it was so exciting, and I really believed that my mother was going to get into the movie. As an adult, I've often wondered what movie they made and if it ever was a hit.

We didn't have many people to say goodbye to when we left Howard Ave. There was a couple, Frances and Sandy, girlfriend and boyfriend, not married. Frances was a calming influence—motherly to my own mother and grandmotherly to me. Frances was the first person I ever met who wasn't born in New York. She was from Frankfort, Kentucky, and she seemed much more sophisticated and worldly than us. I would think of her every time I heard about the Louisville Bats and the Kentucky Derby.

My parents must have kept in touch with Frances and Sandy after we moved out because one day several years later, my father ran into Sandy who told him that his son had lost his leg in Viet Nam. He had only been there for a day. That was the first time I'd heard of Viet Nam, and it wouldn't be the last.

I knew a change was going to come. We were about to move into the brand-new projects called "The Pink Houses" on Linden Boulevard in Brooklyn. I didn't care where we moved, as long as Gramps was coming along for the ride. And he was.

The Mazzine Way of Life

Ninety-six Snedeker Avenue in Brooklyn looked like home sweet home from the outside. If you took a snapshot of the house leaving out the sweater factory on the right and the abandoned boarded up buildings on the left, it could be on the cover of a magazine. The paved walkway led you straight up to a solid brick stoop with a porch as long as the width of the house. Queenie, the Mazzine's dog, was always sitting by the front door to greet you. She was a small, brown mutt who ran the house. To the right of the walkway was my grandfather's prize goldfish pond. This wasn't just a regular little fishpond; this was the size of a small front lawn with a big, beautiful tree standing tall and strong out of a little island in the center. It's bulging roots were begging for more room from the amount of soil it had to offer. I guess years before when it was planted, it was a small tree, but, by the time I was around, it had grown taller than the house, its branches filled with lush green leaves giving shade in the hot summer like an umbrella in the sun. Japanese lanterns were strung on the long strong branches year-round for the many family gatherings held outside. On the roof were the family's prize carrier pigeons housed in elaborate pigeon coops. I'm sure this is something Grandpa Mazzine had started, but by the time I knew him, he didn't go on the roof anymore. The brothers took care of the pigeons that were used for racing and betting on.

A low brick wall surrounded the pond that came right up to the sidewalk. It was filled with a menagerie of fish that ranged from calico carps a foot long to the tiniest goldfish. It even had lily pads. You could not walk by without stopping to take notice of this neighborhood attraction. Some people would just sit on the wall taking it all in. It was my Grandfather Mazzine's pride and joy. He loved hearing the glowing compliments from passersby. Behind the pond was the house my father grew up in. Ten brothers and one sister. They were called the Mazzines, with my grandfather just being called Mazzine. His real name was Anthony. Lucky for me I was named after him when my mother wouldn't let my father name me Perry. That was the Italian tradition for the first grandson.

I've heard different versions of how the Albano family were labeled the Mazzines. The one that I think is closest to the truth is that it's a kind of tribal name of descendants from Sicily. I also learned that if your last name begins with Al, it would be from the time when the Arabs invaded Sicily. Grandpa Mazzine and some of his children looked very middle eastern.

When you stepped over the threshold, the "House

Beautiful" look ended since the house was also an attraction for other activities. Inside was a long, dark hallway; you could hear the original floorboards creaking under your feet. There was a single lightbulb just hanging from a chain, but it was never on. As you walked through, you thought you'd never see light again. You could hear action going on in the dining room ahead. The lit dining room would be the first light you would see, and it was bright. In the walkway, there was so much foot traffic that the linoleum displayed different colors layered over the years; one spot went right down to the wood. This room looked more like a sports bar filled with memorabilia, unlike any traditional Italian dining room I had ever seen. The walls were covered with photos of racehorses, prizefighters, and, most importantly, baseball players. Somewhere on a side wall hung a picture of John F. Kennedy.

Baseball and baseball players, however, held center stage in the Mazzine household as well as in my gramps's life. At the Mazzine's, I was pulled into their love of the game and became familiar with the names of players long before I was in grade school. It was in my blood. There would come a time when one team would become an obsession and an example of my life-long trust that great things happen if you keep on believing. Baseball was their life, and it became mine.

In this distinctive dining room, my grandmother, Josie, held court. Josie was not your typical grandmother.

She had very fair skin, blond hair in a bun, and wore housedresses. Liberated before the '60s, she never wore a bra. I wouldn't know this except for my mother mentioning it. She would say, "Your grandmother is a good-looking woman; she's got skin like a baby's ass, but I don't think she owns a brassiere."

Usually, the sounds of Nat King Cole or Ray Charles would be coming from the back room. My father and I would walk into a haze of smoke, the smell of percolating coffee, and the aroma of Rheingold beer. In the winter there would be hard liquor. The dining room table was large with a plastic tablecloth that looked like a tarp to cover past sins. There was an assortment of ashtrays that fascinated me. I particularly liked the ones with the alligators that would hold the cigarette for you. Unfortunately, it didn't work for some people because there were a lot of cigarette burn marks right through the plastic. I can only imagine this was because of their fascination with the racing form and the excitement of talking sports and sometimes having too much to drink. Surrounding the table was an assortment of mismatched battered chairs of different styles and eras.

Some brothers still lived at home. The tallest of all the short brothers was Uncle Mikey, my godfather. He was always standing around in his own world getting into conversations about conspiracy theories before they were hip. Most of the regulars weren't that interested because they were more focused on drinking and gambling and found Uncle Mikey's ramblings boring, but I saw him as harmless. His main duty was to drink coffee and smoke cigarettes all day. I never saw him sit down. My father's youngest brother, Johnny Boy, was also a regular because he was a change-of-life baby and mentally retarded. I felt sad for him. He was very overweight, had diabetes and open sores on his body. To keep him amused and out of the way, they would just let him drink soda and eat coffee cake all day. I could never really tell his age because he seemed like an overgrown child. When I visited with my father, he was embarrassed and disturbed by the lack of care toward his youngest brother. Sometimes he would openly argue with my grandmother about this, but it always seemed like he was fighting a losing battle.

There were many family gatherings at the Mazzine house throughout the summer. Another uncle was nicknamed called Uncle Polack because he was the only one with blond hair and fair skin and did not look Italian. Unfortunately, he was always inebriated and wanted to stay that way. He would go around to whoever was there and ask if they had any pocket change, which meant he wanted to buy a pint. When he would ask my father for money, my father always said no. When my mother was still visiting the Mazzines, he would go to her, and she would dip into her pocketbook and give him some money. My father would be upset and tell her that he was just going to get a bottle with the money she gave him.

My mother's reply was, "Petie, what else does he have?"

Uncle Polack had fallen down many times and had broken his nose more times than a prize fighter, making it lean to one side of his face. He had cuts and bruises all over his fingers and knuckles, but he was a sweet man. He liked my mother very much, and he would always take out a photograph of himself when he was young and looking good. When he showed my mother, he would say, "Look at me, Mary. They said I looked like Van Heflin."

My mother would say, "You're absolutely right. You were the best looking of all the brothers."

Then he'd stumble off to get another pint. I watched from a window as he weaved his way down the street and I hoped he wouldn't fall. I asked my father how Uncle Polack got this way. He said that a woman broke his heart and he never got over it. He had been drinking ever since. He said, "He turned to the bottle and now the bottle had turned on him."

In this colorful setting, there would be some unrelated regulars—men lining the walls, some with a job, some without a job, some with teeth, some without teeth. Some were running from the law and sometimes they were the "law." If one of the guys hit big on a horse race, there would be more excitement than usual. Of course, if they lost, they'd curse and blame the jockey, calling him a "fucking monkey" and "Why doesn't he go back to Puerto Rico?" The one I liked most was,

"That son of a bitch always wins when I don't bet on him."

There was also a numbers guy called Johnny Numbers. He would come weekly and collect all the nickels, dimes, and quarters that even the old ladies had bet on—the daily numbers before the state lottery came out. Someone would always run out and get the early edition newspaper the night before so they wouldn't have to wait until the morning to see what the number was. Jonny Numbers was always popular.

While all this action was going on in the dining room, my Grandpa Mazzine would be sitting in the living room; it was always very dark, completely different from the room right next to him. He would sit on his cushioned chair and just stare out the window looking at his treasured goldfish pond. Between the darkness and his skinny body sunken in the chair, he'd hardly be noticed, although we could hear him hacking away; he had a terrible smoker's cough. Chesterfield was his brand. You could tell he wasn't happy because he would mumble under his breath when people were too loud. This musky room had a fireplace that was never lit. Above it was an oval photograph of Uncle Jimmy, my father's oldest brother, in his Army uniform. The black and white television was only on if there was a horse race or a baseball game. Other than that, Grandpa Mazzine would listen to the radio that sat on top of the television. It seemed to me that all the other grandchildren were afraid of him, but I wasn't. I would go in and sit next to him in his chair, which easily held both our bodies. Not a man of many words, he would put his arm around me and tell me that I was a good kid. He said that all the other kids who came there ran around like little Indians and bothered his animals. He said, "You're the only one who sits next to me and has manners, just like a little gentleman. Your mother and father are doing a good job."

Grandpa Mazzine loved animals more than people; he was always taking in unwanted pets, and they would run freely in the backyard where he grew grapes for winemaking in his cellar. All the people in the neighborhood knew Mazzine for his love of animals and everyone knew Queenie. He had trained this dog so brilliantly that when you walked into the house Queenie would be there sitting on the porch and the door to the house would be open. If Queenie felt a person didn't belong, she would follow them into the house. That would tip people off that this person didn't belong there. If you were okay with her, she would stay on the porch. I spent a lot of time sitting on the stoop petting and playing with Queenie. I realized that Grandpa Mazzine loved the way I was with his animals.

The Mazzines were either feared or loved, but when they were mentioned, the name always stirred emotions. I noticed that when I left that house, there was always a smell that lingered in my nostrils for a couple of days. I now have come to believe it was the blend of all human vices.

All Come to Look for America

I don't remember leaving Howard Avenue, but I sure do remember moving into the projects. The project housing development on Linden Boulevard in Brooklyn was called the Pink Houses because the buildings were made of pink brick. There were many buildings, but my world consisted of just the one we lived in. It was new and most of the people moving in would be the first tenants. We could still smell the fresh paint that had dried only a few days earlier. We took the elevator to the second floor and walked down the bright yellow cinderblock hall to our apartment. My father had thought of everything. He didn't want us to live on the first floor because those were the ones that would get broken into if there were any break-ins. He didn't want an apartment too close to the elevator where he could hear people coming and going. He didn't mind walking down the hall and picked an apartment that was facing the back side of the building because it looked over the playground, and they could watch me.

Inside and to the right was the living room; I had never seen a living room that big. Straight through was the kitchen; all the appliances were brand new. If you made a left, you'd walk down a hall and first was my parent's bedroom, next was my bedroom, and at the very end of the hall was our bathroom. The first thing my parents did was to take me out the back door of the building where there was a playground; it was a kid's dream. They made me look up and pointed to our apartment and I saw Gramps waving to me. They said, "You see Anthony, when you're in the playground, we'll always be watching you. You just look up and that's where we are."

When I went back inside, we began to set up our new place. I hung out with him while they made plans about how to decorate and where to put the new couch, coffee table, and hi-fi.

The projects were like the UN building—all nationalities and everyone got along and looked out for one another. It was what America was supposed to be all about. We were a community. Couples socialized with other couples, and the kids all played together. Everybody helped everyone else in so many ways. We all had an intriguing story of how we'd come to live in the projects, and everyone was there to make their lives better. At that time, the projects with their low rents were viewed as a steppingstone so that people could save some money and perhaps young couples like my parents could eventually afford to buy a home. Our time there was so much better than in the tenement we had left. To this day, when I smell fresh paint and new construction, I'm back at the projects.

In the front of the building was a big circle of grass and a circle of benches. All the old ladies, who probably weren't that old, would be sitting out there talking and gossiping, and everybody was watching the kids.

I think my father had given up on birds after Perry flew away. So, he went out and bought a ten-gallon fish tank and all the accessories and set up an aquarium. I was excited about this. I couldn't wait to get fish, but my father said the water had to sit for two days to rid the water of chlorine. The two days seemed endless. Finally, my father gave us the okay, and Gramps and I went on our way to bring home some fish.

On our rounds every day, Gramps and I would stop at the pet shop. That would be the last thing before heading for home. I became enthralled with tropical fish, and I learned very quickly all I needed to know. I always wanted to get the livebearers because I wanted to see them have babies, so black mollies and guppies became my favorites. Whenever we got fish for the tank, I asked the man to give me a male and female. As I got older, the man at the pet shop would let me pick out the ones I wanted. The only problem we ran into sometimes was that Gramps would stop at the bar before we got home. It said right on the plastic bag that the fish had to be put into the tank within twenty or thirty minutes or they were not guaranteed. Well, sometimes Gramps would start talking too much to some lady that he met at the bar, and I would start saying, "Gramps, we have to get the fish home."

He'd say, "Don't worry, Champ! If they don't make it, we'll buy new ones tomorrow."

Most of the time, they made it. Sometimes, they didn't. One particular day, he seemed to be talking forever, and I saw my two beautiful mollies gasping for air and their bodies curving, and I kept telling Gramps we had to get home. He told the bartender to call a cab because it took too long to wait for the bus. I thought we were safe.

"Juicy, the cab is here," said the bartender.

We walked out of the bar toward the cab and, just as we got closer, a lady jumped ahead of us.

So, there we were. We had fish and pastries and he had one leg, and he said, "Lady, we called the cab!"

She said, "Sorry, I called one, too."

I never saw Gramps get angry, but he was very upset and said, "Go ahead, Lady, take the cab, but I hope you get a pimple on your ass," and off the cab went. We had to start all over again.

The mollies didn't make it. I had to go into the men's room in the bar and dump them down the toilet. Gramps assured me that tomorrow we'd get new ones, and he wouldn't let this happen again. By the time we got home, my mother was unhappy that we were late. I couldn't tell her that we had fish that died and that we stopped in a bar.

She accused him and he said, "No, Mary, we were going to take a cab and a lady took it, so we had to wait for a new one, and we were late."

I put my two cents in and said, "Gramps said she should get a pimple on her ass," and we all laughed.

She said, "If Petie finds out you're taking him to a bar, he's gonna put an end to you two."

One of the first people we became close to was a neighbor named Betty. She would become another mother figure for my mother, and even though I called her Aunt Betty, a grandmother figure to me. She was Greek with an unmistakable hoarse voice like Ranger Andy, played by Andy Devine on television, and she was wonderful. She had three sons who were very smart. One was in college, one was headed to college, and George, the youngest, was still in high school. They were the first people I ever heard of who were 'going to college.' I didn't know what that meant, but my father always told me, "She has some bright kids. They're gonna go places."

It seemed like Aunt Betty was at our place all the time. She took us under her wing, and we loved it. Her biggest complaint was that she had a husband who went bowling every night. Apparently, he was a great bowler, but Aunt Betty suspected he was doing more than bowling. She would tell my mother that something was going on. One night, when he said he was going bowling, Aunt Betty found his treasured bowling ball and bag in the closet. That was it. She'd had enough. She gathered all his trophies and put them on the table with his bowling bag. We never saw him again. She said, "I threw that son of a bitch out!"

Among the many characters in the building was a man down the hall named Joe. He told my father he was a barber and that if he ever wanted a haircut, he'd give it to him and his son. He persisted in reminding my father of his offer. Finally, my father gave in. I thought getting our haircuts at home was exciting. He sat my father in a chair, put the sheet around him, and said, "Petie, when I get done, you're gonna love it!"

He brought out his scissors and accessories. He gave my father the haircut and asked what he thought of it. My father, I could tell, wasn't happy but didn't want to hurt the guy's feelings.

He said, "Its fine, it's fine."

Then Joe the Barber said, "Mary what do you think of this haircut? Doesn't he look great?"

My mother checked out the new haircut and said, "Petie, I never knew you had such a terrible scar on the back your head."

My father said, "What! You can see my scar? I've been hiding the scar for years. I got it when a cop hit me over the head with the nightstick." He was really disturbed. "I haven't thought about the scar since I had some bit roles in the tv show, *The Untouchables,* as a teenager. They were looking for juvenile delinquents, and they picked us up off the streets and put us in the serial."

I was hearing that for the first time—my father on TV! It made me proud.

Joe then wanted to cut my hair, but my father told him I didn't need a haircut and sent him on his way. Joe never cut my father's hair again.

These were happy days for us. We seemed to be getting along and moving up. We had our own seltzer and syrup delivery, and we could make our own egg creams. I don't know why they called them egg creams because they had nothing to do with eggs, but they were popular in New York. We had a doughnut delivery guy, Dugan's, but the most important move up in our status was that we now had our own Jew. He would knock on our door and peddle household goods that he brought in his trunk. We thought we had the best Jew. More importantly, we were so proud of the fact that he wasn't afraid to come to see us; he had never come to the Howard Avenue neighborhood. He was such a kind, considerate man; he would let my mother and father run a tab until they had the money to pay him. We always looked forward to his visits. We never thought of "Jew" as a derogatory term because when he rang the doorbell and I went to the door, he would say, "Can you go and get your mom, and tell her the Jew is here." We really thought we had made it.

Esther, a yenta, lived in the building. She always wore a house dress. The "girls," my mother included, would play Mahjong with her. She knew everybody's business and that's where all the building's gossip would take place. Esther did her job well.

Downstairs on the first floor, were the Rubins, an elderly couple. I just loved them. If my mother and father were in a pinch and Gramps wasn't around, the Rubins would take me for an hour or so. They were the sweetest, kindest people. Mr. Rubin would get out his accordion and play music for me. He loved it when I would dance to the music holding Mrs. Rubin's hands. I don't know their story or if they had kids or grandkids, but they seemed to be lonely and having a kid in their house really lit them up. Mrs. Rubin always made me cookies. I thought there were no better cookies in the world than hers, and I ate so many. As an adult I realized they were only sugar cookies, but I still say Mrs. Rubin's were the best.

Across the hallway from us was a woman who was raising a teenage daughter on her own, and my father took it upon himself to always keep an eye out for her, too.

Usually, things were peaceful around our building, but one night there was a big commotion outside. Two groups of teenagers were on the street. We could see and hear them from our window, and tempers were flaring. As my father took a closer look, he saw about twenty white teenagers and about twenty black teenagers getting ready for a fight. My father realized one of the boys in the middle of it was the son of a lady who lived in our building.

My father said to my mother, "Mary, you know, he's going out with a colored girl. That's probably what this is about. Let me go see if I can calm things down out there."

My mother was pleading with my father. "Petie, don't get involved They'll turn on you, and what are you going to do when you get down there anyway?"

"Look, I'm just gonna try to help the kid out. You know, he's a good kid. His mother is trying to do the best she can."

None of the other teenagers lived in our projects; they all came from outside the neighborhood. Well, my father walked out there and, as he got to them, my mother was screaming out the window that he shouldn't get involved. But he kept walking. Surprisingly, within minutes he calmed things down, and everybody went home. My father walked that kid back into the building, and there was no fight. They had a little talk. What they talked about I don't know, but I do know I was very proud of my father.

Another man in the building was named Frenchie, and he was responsible for one of the big events of my young life. Frenchie and his wife lived about two floors up from us. He went to the racetrack one day, and he hit a big payday on a horse. He came home and surprised his wife with a color television. This was big. It was the talk of the building. Our circle of friends had all been invited up for the viewing of the first color television in our building. It was done very ceremoniously. We all sat around the television, and everybody had to be quiet; the lights were turned off, and I was in charge of the popcorn bowl probably because I was the only kid there. The picture wasn't perfect, but nobody cared. It was a color television! I will never forget that night. When the lights came on and we were getting ready to leave, we all congratulated Frenchie and his wife on owning this new invention.

Back in my apartment, the hi fi was usually on and music filled the air. It was an interesting mix being that we had three different generations living under the same roof. It felt like it was the "battle of the bands." My mother, who was about twenty, my father, about thirty, and my grandfather, a little over forty, all had different tastes in music and they would defend their era endlessly. The one that all three could agree on was Frank Sinatra. Nobody complained when Sinatra was on.

One bad, but extremely isolated, incident was when I was playing with a little boy my age, and we took turns pushing each other on a little tricycle. The older people were sitting around on the benches in a circle watching the kids. As we played, the boy's teenaged sister came down; she was all dressed up. She saw the imprints of my two dirty hands on the back of his brand-new white shirt and said, "Look what you've done to my brother's shirt! We have to go visiting and you've ruined our holiday."

She slapped me so hard that my teeth chattered. One side of my face was red and burning. I was so surprised I just stared at her. It seemed to be the slap heard around the world because all the people watching were stunned. Some of them were actually yelling at her saying that a teenager shouldn't hit a little kid. Then, she picked me up by the collar and marched me up to her apartment to tell her mother and father what I had done to poor Hershie, but to her surprise, she was the one who got scolded by her parents. While she was trying to convince them why she had done this, they told her to go to her room, and the mother got down on her knees and apologized to me. She said she liked me playing with Hershie, "So please understand that my daughter was wrong to smack you like that and we will punish her."

I just walked away. I knew not to go home and tell my parents or Gramps who would have taken the hinges off the door if anyone would even touch me. Later, I learned it was a Jewish holiday. After the mom apologized to me, I was okay and never told a soul. I thought, better to take the hit rather than escalate the war. I waited for the redness on my face to go away before I went home.

Gramps had become quite the celebrity of the building. He knew everyone and they all called him Mr. Jim. He was in his glory, on top of the world, smiling and waving to everyone. These were happy days for him. As my parents felt more comfortable about leaving us and going out at night, they started socializing, even going frequently to night clubs. My father's friend, Sonny, who I called Uncle Frank, always treated them, and we knew that if we were low, we could always go to Uncle Frank.

Gramps knew that he wasn't allowed to smoke when alone with me; my parents were afraid he would forget a lit cigarette and start a fire. One night when they were out, Gramps and I were having a wonderful time doing what we did best—watching wrestling, playing card games, looking at our fish tank, and I was lighting his cigarettes. Ironically, that night there was a fire in the building and the alarm went off. The fire trucks showed up and the whole building was evacuated. The people were on the sidewalk with boxes of food and treasured belongings.

Gramps said, "We're staying right here. We're not going anywhere, Champ. The walls are fireproof. Nothing is going to happen to us."

We were looking down at everybody and all the people were yelling, "Mr. Jim! Come on down. You'd better get out. Bring Anthony."

He said, "We ain't going anywhere. We have nothing to worry about."

With all the commotion going on downstairs, my parents came home, and the people outside told them that Mr. Jim refused to come down with Anthony. They came flying through the door and were hugging me, making sure I was okay. They asked Gramps what he was thinking. He said the walls were fireproof and we were fine. My parents had jumped to the conclusion that it had to be him who started the fire. After the fire in one of the apartments was put out, all the people went back inside. The fire trucks drove away. Gramps lit a cigarette, since he was allowed to smoke when they were home, and said, "I told you we'd be fine. Those people are crazy!"

My parents had no words. They were mentally exhausted.

Life went on. Gramps and I continued our daily route, always making sure the pet shop was the last stop. That was a must, but we were laying low with the bar scene. I tried never to get Gramps in trouble because he would do anything for me, but one day at the pet shop, while we were going to buy an ornament or fish for the tank, I noticed the cage with rabbits. I'd never seen the rabbits before. I saw this beautiful little black and white bunny, and I lost total interest in the ornament or the fish. I was consumed by the cage with the bunnies, and I told Gramps I wanted one. I named him Fluffy.

You can imagine my mother's reaction to Fluffy. "Dad, what are you, a moron? You bring a rabbit home; we live in an apartment. What are we going to do with a rabbit?"

He said, "Anthony wanted one."

She said, "So you get anything Anthony wants?"

"That's right. Anything Anthony wants, he gets."

"Wait 'til Petie gets home and sees we have a rabbit living in the apartment."

I felt bad that I had gotten Gramps into trouble, but I still wanted the rabbit.

She said to Gramps, "If he told you to jump off the building, would you still jump off the building?"

He said, "Yes, I would. If Anthony wants me to jump off a building, I jump off a building."

"You're both driving me crazy."

Fluffy didn't last long. I knew it wasn't right to have a bunny living in a box in an apartment, so Fluffy went where all unwanted animals go—to Grandpa Mazzine's house. After the scene that caused, I didn't want to ever put my grandfather in that position again. I never wanted to give my mother a reason to put an end to me and Gramps.

In the Italian culture, it is a tradition to visit your grandparents on Sundays. My father thought it would be nice to bring me to visit his parents on Sundays for an hour or two. It was only fair since I spent so much time with my mother's father. Also, I think my father was feeling proud that we were getting ahead and wanted his family to see that. I didn't mind going there; I just minded the dressing up. But there was always a lot of action and animals, and now there was Fluffy.

A Star is Born

At the projects, our lives were humming along. My mother and father were working, saving some money and hoping to buy a house in the future, and Gramps was taking care of me. We had many friends, and everyone was getting along. Mr. Landman, a neighbor who lived down the hall with his wife and two sons told my father about a bungalow colony upstate New York in the town of Monticello in the lower part of the Catskill Mountains. He suggested we go. My parents thought this was a great idea. It would give us a break from the long, hot summer of the city. For a month, we could breathe in the country air and see another side of life, which was something my father wanted for me. Renting summer cottages was popular at the time with city dwellers. We would go up with the Landmans and two or three other couples who were friends of theirs. Mr. and Mrs. Weiner were the owners, and the place was simply called The Weiner's Cottages. We were housed in the bungalow connected to theirs and sometimes when the adults went out, I stayed with Mr. and Mrs. Weiner. I grew to love them, and they treated me as if I were their grandson.

One day a nearby dairy farmer told my father he should come by his farm and make sure he brought his son, Anthony. "There's something he should see, being he's a city kid."

All of the sudden, everything seemed urgent. We had to move fast. There was no time to waste. I had no idea what was going on, but it appeared to me that this was special.

I asked my father about it, and he said, "Just wait, it's a surprise."

When we arrived at the farm, we were led to a barn where a cow was about to give birth. I knew how special a moment it was. We watched as the farmer helped to deliver the baby calf. Giving the mother some distance, we stood in silence at that magical moment. I was filled with awe and amazement, but I left feeling confused when the farmer said, "It's a bull, which means when he's old enough, he'll have to be shipped out of here." It would take me a while to understand and come to terms with this.

I always wanted my parents and especially Gramps to be proud of me. After the summer when we got back to the projects, I started becoming a little performer. Gramps encouraged me with some pocket change to dance for him. He loved saying, "Look at those legs go. I've never seen legs like that in my life."

Great legs and great runners were attributes of the Mazzines. Since music was always playing in our house, it was easy to dance along. My mother was into the teen idol scene and performers like Frankie Avalon, Paul Anka, and Fabian.

Whenever she would put on the song, "Venus," I'd have to slow dance with her because my father made fun of her music and refused to dance to it. I always thought Gramps's taste in music was the hippest. I hadn't found my own sound yet, but I knew it was coming. In the meantime, I would make believe I had a microphone in my hand and sing along like I was Frank Sinatra or Tony Bennett. Of course, when I did Frank Sinatra, they all enjoyed that. Then I got into imitating people on television. This would get me the most rounds of applause because I was getting pretty good at my new craft while studying people's characteristics on television. I performed, not only for my parents and Gramps, but for the neighbors who my parents invited to see me put on a little show. Now this, I liked! I realized this was the way to go.

A classic moment took place one night when Gramps and I got tired of hearing my mother say how beautiful she was and how everybody in the hat department said she looked like Elizabeth Taylor. We were rolling our eyes. Now that I was a 'star,' I thought I would have a little fun. When they were all in the living room, I went into my mother's bedroom, took out one of her dresses, put it on, then her shoes and one of her famous sparkling hats, and I got an extra pair of eyeglasses. I found a cigarette holder left there from a costume party and came prancing into the living room, saying, "Everyone tells me I look like Elizabeth Taylor, don't you think? You know, not everyone could sell hats. You have to have a face like mine." I was pretending to smoke from the cigarette holder, and my father and grandfather started cracking up, thoroughly enjoying my impression. My mother seemed startled then upset that my father and grandfather thought this was so funny.

She said, "This is why this kid has no respect for me." But then she began to laugh and cry at the same time, and the coffee she was drinking was coming out of her nose.

In the early '60s, my parents took me to Manhattan to see the opening of a movie. They wanted me to experience things that they hadn't as children. This was a life-changing event for me. The movie was "West Side Story." We went with our Jewish friends. I mention this because having these Jewish people as friends added culture to our lives and exposure to the arts, including Broadway plays and concerts. Their influence in our lives was profound. As a kid, I was taking all this in.

When the movie started and my mother saw that the story was about gangs, she was conflicted about whether it was appropriate for someone my age. She really was trying her best as a parent. But I was riveted. Nothing had ever impacted me like that in my six years of life. I was blown away by the music and tough guys dancing. To this day, when I hear the opening sound of "West Side Story," the hair on my arms stands up. Shortly after that, they bought the album, and since I was the DJ at the apartment, I played it continuously and memorized the songs that I really loved. I decided to add the songs to my repertoire for my little show for the neighbors. They would get a kick out of me singing, "When You're a Jet," and "Officer Krupke." They would laugh hard when I would sing, "No one wants a fella with a social disease." I didn't understand the meaning of the sentence, but if they laughed, I would sing it.

By that time, my mother had gotten over being angry about me imitating her as Elizabeth Taylor and now encouraged it. So, my father would bring more neighbors to see my show, and the grand finale was me imitating my mother. As the applause got louder and the small group grew, I was eating it up and gaining in confidence. I realized this was the kind of attention I wanted. My father was excited and was inviting more people to see my act. I was becoming more popular than the neighbor who bought the first color television.

Aunt Betty was my biggest fan. After the show when things calmed down, I would still have my little job of walking her upstairs to her apartment and brushing her hair so she would be able to go to sleep. I swear, I would be able to put her to sleep in three minutes. My mother and father felt bad that I accepted a quarter from her because they felt I didn't spend enough time, but I asked them, "What can I do if she falls asleep so quickly?"

When I was about to enter first grade at St. Fortunata, a Catholic school, I was afraid that my daily life with Gramps was coming to an end. We had a little talk, and he told me that the fun wasn't over and that he would be waiting for me when I came home. He assured me that we were just going to move our time together to evenings and weekends.

My parents were determined that their only child would not be spoiled and put all their efforts into raising me right—with manners and respect. They wanted me to have a good, disciplined education. But my mother was a woman of many fears, perhaps because her mother left her at an early age. When she primed me for my first day of school, she acted as if it was going to be a traumatic experience. On that day, I calmly put on my new uniform. My mother was hysterical. I didn't understand why this was affecting her so strongly. When we got to the school, I saw many other children crying and clutching their mothers. They didn't want to let go. I just kissed my mother on the cheek and walked in.

Just as she had promised, my mother was at the door when I got out of school. When we got home, Gramps was there, then my father came home. They asked my mother how my first day was. She said, "It's unbelievable. He was the only kid not crying. He walked into the school as if he didn't even love me."

Some of my mother's fears might have been justified, but I don't think she should have been sharing them with me at five years old. During the Cuban missile crisis, my mother had me thinking that we were going to be attacked any day, and she was frightened with Castro and Khrushchev claiming that war was imminent. Once again, Gramps reassured me and said that if anything happened, we were in the safest place in the world. These projects were built like a fallout shelter. Whenever my mother would have various fears, Gramps would help lay them to rest in a way only he could.

In my building, there was kid named Ritchie who had a terrible skin condition all over his arms. I had never seen anything like it. It was more than a rash. It was more like red, inflamed scabs, and I told my mother that nobody played with this kid because of the way he looked. She said, "Yes, don't go near him. You may catch it."

Hearing that, Gramps told me privately not to worry, that I wouldn't catch anything, and that, since Richie had no friends, he was the kid he wanted me to play with. So, I did hang out with Ritchie, and every time his arms brushed against me, I made sure I didn't flinch to make him feel like an outcast. I was remembering that I had a retarded uncle and a cousin who was a dwarf, and I just had to have more compassion. No matter what it took to play with him, I would not make him feel alone.

In 1960, there was a lot of excitement in the house. My mother was voting for the first time because she was twenty-one. Gramps and I were cheering her on days before she went to the polling station letting her know how proud we were of her.

After she voted, she came through the door and said, "Anthony, give me a hug. I just voted for the first time." We asked who she voted for and my father jumped in saying that was a private matter, but she blurted out, "I voted for Kennedy because he's so good-looking!"

Tony's parents (right) at the Town and Country Nightclub on one of their many nights out, with his brother Frank and his wife.

Tony was a happy only child living in the projects with Gramps taking care of him, before his mother became a hypochondriac.

Tony's mother, Cousin John, and Tony (left).
Happy times living at the projects.

The Godfather

Frank Pantano was my father's best friend and mentor when I was growing up. Everybody called him Sonny, a nickname that matched his pleasant, easygoing disposition and warm smile perfectly. On his business card, you'd find the name Sonny Parker. One of his many traits was to reveal as little as possible to people who were not in his inner circle. My story would not be complete without mentioning this man, who I called Uncle Frank out of respect. His influence and impact on my father enabled me to live a much different life than the other Mazzine children, my cousins. Uncle Frank was like a character from an old mobster movie; with his hair meticulously combed back, he looked just like George Raft. He dressed in a suit with a starched handkerchief in his top pocket that matched the suit. Dapper and mysterious, he was always a gentleman, especially in front of the ladies. Uncle Frank had class, and he also had a stammer, which softened his George Raft image a bit. He was street smart like my father's brothers, but unlike the Mazzines, he was not rough around the edges. He could fit into all situations and any group of people. He would be welcome in the most high-class restaurants and night clubs as an upstanding citizen. He was accepted in society and followed its rules, but he also could walk into the Mazzine house any time of the day and be right at home, and he knew the game of the street. Uncle Frank, who was about ten years older than my father and treated him like his kid brother. My father learned a lot from him and picked up many good habits.

The Mazzines were good people with kind hearts, but lived a wayward, gypsy existence. They would give you the shirt off their backs. It was one for all and all for one. Uncle Frank demonstrated to my father how to live a more normal, mainstream life by being responsible and bringing home his pay rather than gambling it away, working a steady job or two, paying bills on time, and building up credit so that in the future he could buy a house. Little by little, my father became the black sheep of the Mazzine family. His brothers considered him too straight and too conservative. But I will be forever thankful for how my father turned out with the help of Uncle Frank.

Uncle Frank taught my father to live responsibly. One of the habits he taught my father was to show up for an appointment ten minutes early. That stayed with my father for the rest of his life. Uncle Frank always seemed to have money and was very generous with it. He often took my parents out to nightclubs and for nights on the town in Manhattan, which was great for me and Gramps. Uncle Frank always had different girlfriends with him. My favorite was named Sarah; she had red hair and was a lot of fun. I remember him teasing her in the car.

Once my father told me, "You know, your Uncle Frank treats all his girls wonderfully. One he put through college, and for one, he fixed all her teeth. When Uncle Frank likes you, you'll be treated with kindness."

For all the years I knew him, at a certain time each day, he had to go into Manhattan. No matter where he was, no matter what the situation, he would say goodbye and be on his way to meet the night and take care of business. The only time I remember him not going to Manhattan was in the winter. He would go to Miami and that always meant a crate of oranges would be delivered to our door. When he was in Miami, my father would take care of business for him in New York. Whenever my father would leave the house, he would tell my mother, "Mary, I'm doing Frank a favor, and it pays well." She was okay with that. When my father did anything with or for Uncle Frank, my mother was okay with it, unlike if he got too involved with the Mazzines.

Uncle Frank lived with his older brother, Mike, and his sister-in-law, Fanny, who owned a two-story apartment building in Queens and lived on the top floor. He had a room there and came and went as he pleased. Fanny was, without question, the kindest, most cheerful person, without sin, that I've ever met in my life. She was deeply religious, and in front of their house was a statue of the Virgin Mary, but I didn't think they needed that because there was no one more saint-like than Aunt Fanny. She went to Mass every morning; there should have been a shrine outside for her. She would become another of my adopted grandmothers. Her husband Mike was a quiet, unassuming man with a big belly, and always sat in a reclining chair. He had the thickest eyeglasses I've ever seen in my life. They were like Coke bottles, and by the time I came along, he had a heart condition. His biggest form of entertainment was going to burlesque shows to see strip teases. Aunt Fanny would take it all in jest and say, "Oh, he's not hurting anyone. I let him have his fun. Besides, he tells me it's good for his heart."

Aunt Fanny loved the Beatles and when we went there on Sundays, she'd be singing "I Wanna Hold Your Hand" while she was putting food on the table. Of course, I'd have to sing along with her. My father, who couldn't stand the Beatles, said, "The Beatles couldn't shine Perry Como's shoes. In a year, no one will know who they are." We always stayed to watch Ed Sullivan with her on Sunday nights and then go home when it was over.

Aunt Fanny's brother also lived with them. This man was more mysterious than Uncle Frank! I only saw him twice in my life; he was quiet and hardly ever there. He was always traveling. Now I realize that he was a real live cowboy in Brooklyn. He would travel in the rodeo circuit, and one time I remember my parents letting me take off from school to see him in a rodeo with Uncle Frank and Sarah, his girlfriend. I was fascinated. The second time I met him, I looked into the cowboy's room. I didn't want to intrude on his privacy, but he invited me in and started showing me all his trophies and belt buckles while he was putting on his cowboy boots. He always walked out with his cowboy hat in his hand. I was amazed. I never knew his name. They all lived in the same household—the most religious, saintly woman I ever met and her husband, who spent his days at burlesque shows, one mobster who had to go to Manhattan every night to take care of business, and a real live cowboy who did the rodeo circuit!

Uncle Frank had one of the most interesting ways of giving people birthday gifts. He had no time for shopping and had no kids in his life other than me. He kept quarters, half dollars and silver dollars in separate sewing tins. His way of giving a birthday gift was to offer you a choice of which tin you would like to dip into. The challenge was to pick the tin that would bring you the most amount of money. I didn't like the quarters because too many of them would slip out of your hand. You probably would be able to get the most money with half dollars, but being intrigued with coins from an early age, I liked dipping into the silver dollars because they stopped making them in 1935. So, when it was my birthday, he would say, "Anthony, which tin do you want me to bring out?" I would always pick the silver dollars.

But there were rules. You couldn't scoop. You could only use one hand. And, when he counted to three, the cover would be put down and whatever you got out of it was yours and whatever was left was his. I would get excited even when it wasn't my birthday, and I would watch my mother or another person dipping into a tin. It would be a big ceremony before the tin would come out. You didn't want to pester him about taking out the tin and, believe me, he would keep you waiting until just before he would leave for Manhattan. Sometimes, I would get lucky, and Aunt Fanny would tell Uncle Frank to take out the tin. He would object saying that it was not a birthday, but she kept at it.

She'd say, "Sonny, he's just a kid. Let him have some fun."

There was no way to refuse Aunt Fanny who was such a sweet person, so out came the tin and I would get to dip, even when it was not my birthday.

Then, when he would leave, she would say, "He only does that for Anthony, no one else; I knew I'd get him to do it if I kept asking."

I think the most I ever got was around twenty dollars, but I heard that there was a lady named Virginia, who they said had hands like a man, and she held the unofficial record for thirty-five dollars.

When I was about twenty years old, Uncle Frank, who was getting ready to go out for the evening, called me into his room as he combed back his hair and put on his suit. He said, "Oh, let me show you something before I go out," and he showed me a beautiful little two-shot Derringer gun. He looked down at me and said, "Anthony, I only had to use this once in my life. A man got too rough with one of my girls, and I had to shoot him in the back of his head." It was then that I realized that all the "girlfriends" who I had met over the years were not girlfriends; they were prostitutes. I still say Sarah was my favorite. It's hard to believe that Uncle Frank's influence on my father altered the way I would live my entire life, and that influence was about to pay off.

The American Dream

My mother's sister Jeanette and her husband Funzi (short for Alphonso) bought their first home in Rosedale, Queens. Aunt Jeanette, like my mother, was blessed with good looks, a different look from my mother, but beautiful just the same—olive skin, big brown eyes, and jet-black hair. Their looks were perhaps a small consolation for the unhappy childhoods they both had. Unlike my mother, Aunt Jeanette married the son of hardworking Italian immigrants. They were model citizens, a totally different family than the Mazzines. Uncle Funzi was a fireman.

During the early 1960s, we visited Aunt Jeanette and her growing family often. She already had two boys and one on the way. Her oldest, John, was four years younger than me, and we got along like he was my younger brother. We would grow to be close and share many memorable moments. In the end, Aunt Jeanette had five boys never giving birth to the daughter she had always wished for. My mother and she were getting along fine as long as the topic of their mother didn't come up. Their main point of contention was that my aunt dreamed of being reunited with her mother. My mother, on the other hand, didn't want any part of it. The reason for their differences might have been that when Theresa left, Aunt Jeanette was only two and had no memories of her. My mother was five and remembered with bitterness the promise to be home for Christmas that Theresa did not keep.

Unbeknownst to me, my parents had begun to look for a place of their own nearby. The projects had been good to us, and it worked out just the way it was supposed to. Living there gave them a chance to save some money and, with addition of the GI Bill, it made it possible to buy their first home and step into the American Dream. They soon found a house just a block away from Aunt Jeanette's. One block the other way was a beautiful park with two lakes and many baseball fields. My parents showed me the neighborhood and explained where I would go to school—PS138. I had many emotions. I was happy we would have a house with a yard and live right up the street from my cousins, but I was going to miss our life in the projects. It was such a beautiful, wonderful, fun, and happy time, and it was coming to an end. The familiar was safe and the unknown, even though it looked good, was a little scary.

As our neighbors in the project learned we were moving, one by one they stopped by to wish us luck. Some were just neighbors, some were friends, and some had become family. With my father's brothers, we had all the help we needed to move. The night before we were to go, Aunt Betty and my mother were in the

kitchen wrapping dishes and silverware. They started reminiscing about all the good moments we had shared over the years.

"Remember when Anthony put on his little shows for us?"

"Remember when Mr. Jim would not leave the building when the fire broke out?"

"Remember when George lost Anthony at the beach?"

They were crying and laughing at the same time.

I tried to put on a happy face about moving, but inside I was so sad. It was the end of an era. I would miss so many people, but, most of all, I'd miss Aunt Betty. At that moment, I dropped a little dish to the floor, and it broke into a hundred little pieces. I began to cry uncontrollably. My mother and Aunt Betty tried to assure me that it was just a little dish, and it didn't matter. They asked me what was wrong. I was so upset. The three of us hugged, and then I let it out, "When we move, who will brush Aunt Betty's hair?"

Believing

After the tearful goodbyes at the projects in the summer of 1962 just before the school year started, we moved into our first house in Rosedale, Queens. Even though we still lived in New York City, it seemed like our own little, small town. In miles, it wasn't too far from the projects in Brooklyn, but it was a whole new world. Rosedale had everything a young boy could dream of, and I was familiar with the neighborhood because we had visited Jeanette and Funzi so many times.

We lived on 145th Avenue. It was the third house from the corner. On the corner was a library. On the opposite side was the post office. Everything you needed was within three blocks. You could walk to all the stores; you never had to leave your little hometown. On my block, like all the other blocks, there were ten houses on each side. They all looked alike except for the colors people painted them. When we first moved into the house, a truck pulled up and on it was a huge picnic table with the benches attached. My father and two other men carried it to our back patio, and my mother said, "Petie, where did this come from?"

He said, "It fell off a truck."

Right there on the wood was engraved *Property of the City of New York.*

She said, "Are you crazy? You could lose your job for this!"

His answer was, "Mary, don't worry. The City sent us a housewarming gift."

At the time, my father worked for the City of New York in the Highway Department and also had a side job in the evenings to keep the bills paid.

When you're the new kid on the block, the other kids ask you where you moved from. I would just say Brooklyn, not the projects, because they wouldn't understand. They would ask what my religion was, and I'd tell them Catholic. They would ask what nationality and I would say Italian. Some of them had never met an Italian kid before. Until we moved there, it was basically a German/Irish community, and some of the older people who had been there since there were potato farms on the land were a little concerned with the "Italian invasion." Some didn't think Italians were white. They also thought we might have Mafia ties— which we did—and that we would be loud—which we were—and that we would have a lot of company with family visitors—which we had—and that their property value would go down—which it did not. The only way you could tell the houses of the Italians from the neighbors' houses was they had a little black jockey statue on their lawns holding a lantern, and we had some kind of Catholic saint or a birdbath. This was the first time that I felt prejudice from some people, but they got over it pretty quickly, and it's a good thing they did because many more Italians would move into the neighborhood in the next couple of years.

In September of 1962 1 started second grade at P.S.138. It was the first time I had ever gone to a public school, and I felt a little ahead of the other kids in my class, so the nuns must have done a good job at the Catholic school. My first teacher there was a thin, elderly woman who probably was in her final years of teaching. I don't think the other kids realized she was a drinker, but I could tell because I'd seen a lot more of life than they had.

When my teacher wanted a drink, she would announce to the class that she had a cold and needed some cough medicine. Then she would open the coat closet, reach into her pocket, and take a swig. Usually the more swigs she took, the nicer and more sentimental she became. She would take out photographs of her family and have the class sit around her desk as she passed the photos around. But there were times when her mood shifted. One of those times, her mood shifted to impatience and downright meanness. She headed toward a girl's desk. I always felt for this girl because she was overweight and unkempt and wore outdated clothes; it was clear that she didn't have an easy life. That day, the teacher took out her frustrations by pulling this girl's hair and screaming at her. She just would not stop. I knew I had to make a decision quickly. Do I respect the teacher under all circumstances like my parents and Gramps taught me? Or do I stand up for the downtrodden and abused people? Just then the Mazzine side took over, and, as I got up to protect the girl and stop this violence, the principal walked in. The teacher tried to compose herself and the principal said, "I'll meet you in my office." That moment stands out in my mind so vividly and I'm sure it also does for that girl.

Otherwise, my life in our new home couldn't have been better. It was great to see my mother and her sister becoming closer after many years of living separately. I had new friends and Gramps was always around, sitting on the stoop or in the backyard. Who could imagine that two uneducated people coming from the backgrounds my parents did would be in this situation? My parents were making new friends quickly; everyone seemed to be in the same boat. Nobody was rich, nobody was poor. Everybody was just proud that they owned their homes and were trying to raise their children the right way.

I was meeting kids my own age, and it was easy to make friends. There were four boys on the corner, one boy a block away. Across the street was a family with one boy older than me and a set of twins my own age—a boy named Victor and a girl named Miriam. Of all the kids, Miriam was the one I'd say was my first real friend. She was the ultimate tomboy with her boyish bobbed haircut and cute little freckles. Sometimes she wore eyeglasses, and she was some great little athlete.

Miriam went to a Catholic school. We only saw one another after school and weekends. We were inseparable from the beginning. Interestingly enough, her twin brother, Victor, was much more fragile than she was. In the first game we made up, Matt, her older brother, was a scientist—something he actually wanted to be. Victor was the hunter in his safari hat and carried a toy rifle. Miriam and I were chimpanzees—Jocko and Candy. Victor, the hunter, wanted to cage us and bring us back for trophies, and Matt, the scientist, would always come and save us if we were caught and caged. It was a fight between good and evil. Sometimes when we hid, it would take hours for Victor to find us, but we'd always get rescued in the end. Hiding gave Miriam and me a chance to bond as friends. One time, we hid behind my garage, a good spot. It was very dark there; the ground was moist, and the evergreen trees could cover us. We decided to write a note saying we had been there at that moment, put it in a bottle, and bury it for future civilizations to find. Somewhere, behind that garage is the note that Miriam and I left. I often dream of going back one day and looking for it. When choosing sides for games, I always wanted Miriam on my team. We were the kind of friends that parents would say, "When these two get older, they're gonna fall in love and get married."

That first Christmas we had surprise guests. For the first and only time in my life, Grandpa and Grandma Mazzine left their house to visit us. Since neither one of them drove, my father picked them up and brought them home. They even brought my mentally retarded uncle, Johnny Boy. It was the first time I ever saw my two grandparents in the same room and even then, I did not hear them speak a word to one another. Grandpa Mazzine was all smiles, so proud of my father's new accomplishment. I'm sure Grandma Mazzine was happy also, but she seemed so out of place, missing the comfort of her gambling den.

When winter came, my father became obsessed with shoveling the snow on our sidewalk. Not only our sidewalk, but the whole block's sidewalk. He took great joy in waking up early and shoveling our side of the street. The neighbors loved that, especially if they were old. He would make sure that their paths were always clear. My mother always said, "Petie, you're gonna die of a heart attack. Don't you know you're in the heart attack age zone?"

His reply would be, "Don't worry, Mary. I took a shot of whiskey. It keeps you warm. It keeps your heart pumping."

The holiday season, Christmas Eve and Christmas Day, was held at my Aunt Jeanette's house. Aunt Jeanette was my Santa Claus. She bought me so many gifts every year. Christmas, however, would always have a recurring theme. Even though Gramps still had his swagger, the holiday Christmas music would start to play, and it would bring back the memories of his wife's leaving him right before Christmas. The song, "I'll be Home for Christmas," would bring him to tears, and he'd start talking about his wife. My mother would get furious and tell Gramps that Theresa was nothing but a tramp and she hoped she would die a long, painful death so she could spit on her grave. At the time, Aunt Jeanette would keep her feelings to herself, but we all knew how she felt. This would be a volatile topic for the two sisters for the rest of their lives. It would fracture their relationship, and at times they wouldn't speak to one another, even though they lived a block away. Nobody was better at hurting somebody with words than my mother. She still was the Queen of Venom.

Gramps always believed that his wife was going to come home someday, especially, around Christmas. He never stopped believing and he instilled in me the idea to never stop believing. He would tell me to look at how he had made a comeback in 1955. It was his miracle year when I was born and finally his Brooklyn Bums became world champs. Until the end, he was a true believer. Thank God, the blues only lasted a short time every year, and Gramps was back in his groove right after Christmas.

If Christmas gave Gramps a rough time, there was another family tradition that was rough for me. It took place every March when the circus came to town. My mother and father had been taking me to the circus ever since I could remember. It was the big one, Barnum and Bailey's Ringling Brothers at Madison Square Garden. My mother would always look so glamorous, and my father would be dressed up too; we really looked like the American Dream. There was one problem with this: I hated the circus! Nothing made me sadder than that one day a year at the circus. When we toured the animals and I could see the chains on elephants' legs and their heads swaying back and forth, and the tigers in their cage, pacing, everybody except me was so thrilled to be up close. I thought it was terrible to have these animals caged and chained. The year I was eight, I thought an elephant had caught my eye, in particular, and was talking to me about this terrible life he was living. Then, there were the clowns—I found nothing more depressing than watching clowns do their tricks. One time after the show the clowns showed themselves taking off their makeup and costumes. Up to that point, I had never thought of them as real people. I also took it very personally knowing some were midgets and dwarfs because of my cousin Joanne's dwarfism.

Finally, when I was ten, I spoke up and told my parents I didn't want to go. They were stunned. They both said that I loved the circus. I told them that *they* loved the circus and that I didn't want to spoil their fun, but please, I found it much too depressing. That was the end of the family tradition of taking me to the circus. They still couldn't believe it and thought I was strange. They would say, "What kid doesn't like to go to the circus? Every kid loves to go to the circus. You should be happy that you have such wonderful parents who want to take you."

Thinking back, maybe my parents were right. I was a little odd. For example, I never read a comic book in my life, thought cartoons were silly, and every Easter, when every kid was waiting to get a chocolate bunny, I preferred white chocolate. Gramps made sure I would have the biggest white bunny of all times. Maybe I was a little different than the regular kid, however, I found taking care of my aquarium and my tropical fish much more interesting than other traditional "boy" activities. I would check out any book from the library on tropical fish so I could learn more. I had a lot of Grandpa Mazzine in me when it came to loving animals.

One time, I went to my favorite pet shop in Newberry's Department Store. I had enough money to buy two black mollies. I always wanted to get a male and a female and I had them picked out, but I had a dilemma that day because I also saw a baby in the tank, and I wanted that one also, but I only had money for two fish. The salesgirl sensed my frustration, and, when I told her my dilemma, magically, she told me not to worry. She would just throw the baby in and when I went to the cashier, he wouldn't notice that there was an extra fish in there. I thought this incident showed what Gramps meant by being "a believer." I believed so hard that my little dream came true! It was pure magic. I have never stopped believing.

My Own Team

Baseball always had a special place in the hearts of both sides of the family. My grandfather Mazzine had been such a baseball fanatic that he was named the Number One Fan of the New York Giants in 1936. He appeared in every major New York paper before the World Series when he waited in line to be the first person in the stadium. I'm happy my father saved the newspaper clippings for me.

He dreamed of having his own baseball team and it came true when he had ten sons. They even had their own uniforms printed with the logo, "The Albano Brothers." They played in the tri-state area. I have one photograph of them beating another team of brothers in Long Branch, New Jersey with a score of two to one. Grandpa Mazzine always carried a little black book of the official rules of baseball. If you wanted to debate him and make bets about baseball, he would be coy at first, but then when he knew he had you, he would take out his book and prove his case and you'd lose the argument and your money. So, naturally, after we settled into our new neighborhood, my father signed me up for Little League that summer.

The highlight of being in the Little League was a field trip to see the New York Mets play at the Polo Grounds. My father was excited about this because that's where his New York Giants had played all those years. It brought back a lot of memories of his youth and the many times he had spent afternoons at the park, and now I was going to the same park where he grew up. That was a day I'd never forget; it was the day I fell in love with my own team—the New York Mets. I wasn't aware at that moment that in several years, I would still be in love with the Mets and also in love with a woman who would share the most exciting magical baseball year of all time with me.

When I came home my father couldn't wait to hear about my experience going to my first Major League baseball game. I told him that the Mets lost, as usual, but I loved everything about it—the smell of the grass, the people chanting "Let's go Mets!" the homemade banners that people waved. Being there was pure fantasyland for me. He was happy that I got to see the Polo Grounds before it got torn down. After that season, the Mets would be moving into their brand-new home, Shea Stadium in Flushing Meadows, Queens. I couldn't believe they were moving to my borough of New York. It would be right next to where the 1964 World's Fair would be. Things were changing.

After I went to my first baseball game, I would watch or listen to every inning of every game possible. The more the Mets lost, the more I loved them. I don't know if Gramps was a Mets fan because of me or he was becoming a fan on his own. Either way, I knew I would soon win him over. With this new team in town, the only National League team since the Dodgers and Giants left, the Mets didn't have any star players. They seemed to find every imaginable way to lose a game, even when it didn't seem possible that they could lose. But they were never unloved. In 1963, they would attract over one million fans even though they didn't have their own stadium yet and would only win fifty-one games and lose 111. I wanted to learn everything I could about my new team. It is said that in 1962, their first year, they lost an amazing 120 games and were considered the worst team ever to take a field calling themselves a major league team. The players in the early years of the Mets were people that other teams wanted to get rid of or were too old and should have been retired or too young and not quite ready to be in major leaguers. Ask most kids on the street who their team was, and they'd probably say the Yankees. If you asked them their favorite player, it would always be Mickey Mantle. But that was too easy for me. I'd rather be loyal to a team who needed me.

The Mets were responsible for my father and Gramps talking a lot more about baseball. My father was still claiming that he could never love baseball again because the Giants deserted him. Gramps would always say that about his Dodgers who left, but he was coming around. Of course, in my house, to say that you were a Yankee fan would be considered treasonous. It was unheard of. My father loved to tell me stories about his Giants and going down the list of the stars that he saw play, his favorite being Willy Mays, and Gramps would tell me about "the Brooklyn Bums" and Jackie Robinson. Interestingly enough, Gramps's favorite baseball player was Roy Campanella. Roy Campanella's career ended when he was in a car accident that left him paralyzed from the waist down. I used to think that Gramps empathized with him because he was missing a leg and related to what Campanella was going through. My father was so anti-Yankee that when Roger Marris hit sixty-one home runs, my father said it didn't count because Babe Ruth hit sixty home runs in a shorter season when they played only 154 games in one year. With the Mets, I found a missing piece of my life; I now had my own team. They even had a nickname for people like me. We were called "the new breed." The Mets manager, Casey Stengel, called them "The Amazing Mets." Some people said they were amazing because of how badly they played and how often they lost.

In that same year of my first Mets game, I would hear Peter, Paul and Mary for the first time singing "If I Had a Hammer," "Puff the Magic Dragon," and "Blowin' in the Wind." I had found the sound and style of music that I love still. It was music that not only had a great melody but was trying to bring about social change. Now I had my music—folk music. At

that point, I didn't know Bob Dylan wrote "Blowin' in the Wind." I didn't even know who Bob Dylan was. That would come later. Until I heard that song, my regular routine before I went to school was to go to the basement to feed my fish and to listen to one song on the hi-fi from the album "West Side Story." I would always select a different song to get me in the mood to meet the day, a habit that has stayed with me until now. I do not leave the house without listening to one song. Soon, I would discover songwriters. My life seemed complete. I now had Miriam, my mollies, music, and the Mets.

Brooklynite, Bent on Being No. 1 Series Fan, Has Camped at Polo Grounds for 12 Days

Tony Albano, a hardy baseball fan from Brooklyn, where the breed, of necessity, is hardier than any other species in the United States, is not going to miss being the first bleacherite through the turnstiles at the Polo Grounds tomorrow morning.

This gentleman, who lives at 96 Snediker Avenue, Brooklyn, has made sure of that by camping at the very edge of the Eighth Avenue entrance since Friday, Sept. 18.

He was discovered and interviewed there yesterday, while seated firmly in a small swivel chair, rather ornate for such a purpose. The No. 1 fan usually reposes on a dry-goods box during his long vigil.

"I got to the Polo Grounds on Sept. 17 in 1933," said Albano with serious dignity. "But that year I only got fourth place in line. This year there ain't gonna be no doubt about it—I'm No. 1."

He is accompanied by a young Negro friend, William McCoy, of 2,551 Atlantic Avenue, Brooklyn, who actually arrived there first.

"But," explained Albano, "he's gonna be No. 2 because I'm buying the food for us while we wait."

Albano is very jealous of his exalted position as the 1936 World Series No. 1 bleacherite, as evidenced when photographers appeared.

"No, sir," he said emphatically when the cameramen prepared to snap McCoy with him. "He ain't gonna be in any picture. I'm the No. 1 fan and I want my picture alone."

So Albano was shot solo—unless some of the photographers played a mean trick on him.

The New York Times
Published: September 29, 1936
Copyright © The New York Times

NY Times *article on Grandpa Mazzine being honored in 1936 as the Number One Fan of the New York Giants baseball team.*

Grandpa Mazzine, the manager (last on right), achieved his dream of having nine sons in uniform on his own baseball team, 1947.

Tony's father being welcomed home from the army by Grandpa Mazzine, and Tony's grandmother Josie.

Gramps on his wedding day with Theresa, the grandmother Tony never met, who five years later would leave him and her two daughters.

The End of the Innocence

September came around again, and I had a lovely new teacher, Mrs. Jameson. She was everything you would want in a teacher—kind and soft-spoken—and I have never forgotten her. Soon after the school year began, she asked us all to come dressed for Halloween in costume. She was going to select one boy and one girl as the winners. I was doing okay in school and my parents were happy that I liked my teacher. I asked my parents what I should go as. The three of us decided I should get dressed up as a girl, just the way I used to imitate my mother. I did. I put on the dress, the earrings, the hat with the dangles, and my mother's shoes and off to school I went. Mrs. Jameson could not stop laughing or hide the surprise on her face when I showed up as a girl—she immediately announced that I was the winner in the "boy" department and then announced the winner of the girls. She sent the winners to two other classrooms to show us off. When I got to the first classroom, the other teacher, who didn't know me, asked what I came as?

I said, "I'm a girl."

She said she knew that, but what did I come as?

I said, "I came as a girl."

She said she was a little confused; she assumed I was a girl. Finally, I took off my hat and said, "No, I am a boy."

She was shocked, and then she hugged me and said, "Now I know why Mrs. Jameson picked you as the winner." All the teachers thought this was terrific, and I was a hit on Halloween. Little did I know the fun and games would end very quickly. My world was about to be rocked.

One day my mother was playing with one of her nephews at Aunt Jeanette's house and realized that she couldn't hear the ticking of her own watch from one ear. She was alarmed. She made an appointment with an ear, nose, and throat specialist. The doctor found that she had a tumor in her inner ear, which had to be operated on and removed. My parents prepared me by saying that my mother was going to have to be in the hospital but that everything was going to be fine. I would see her in maybe five or six days. My parents were always good about keeping their promises, so I just went along with the program. Around November 20th, my father was going to take my mother to the hospital, and I remember her telling me she would see me one day next week and to be good for all the people who would be taking care of me, including Gramps. As I hugged her goodbye, she said to me, "I told the doctor I can't die because I have a little boy at home, and he needs a mother. I didn't have a mother so it's even more important to me that he has one."

I was comforted to have Gramps with me, and actually thought that now we would have more fun than usual. But, on Friday, November 22nd, almost at the end of the school day, Mrs. Jameson, who always had such composure, said that she had some very bad news for us. She said that the president had been shot. As she sat down in her chair, she said that all of us must go directly home, and she started crying and put her head on the desk. During that era, everybody listened to what their teachers told them, and we all went directly home. Since no one expected us to get out early, on this rare occasion there was no one home when I got there.

Since my mother was being operated on that day, my father had arranged for our next-door neighbor, Mrs. Cleveland, to take me into her house if he was late getting home from the hospital. I listened to what the teacher said and went from school directly to Mrs. Cleveland's, who I really didn't know other than to say hello. I'd never been in her house; it was very cluttered and looked like nothing had changed in decades. She was a nice enough lady, but you could tell she hadn't had an easy life. I think she raised her two children on her own and by this time they were out of the house. There was no Mr. Cleveland. As I sat in her living room, she had the television on and it was announced that the president had, indeed, died. Even though I was probably there only about an hour, time moved very slowly while I waited for my father to come get me.

For the rest of the weekend, my father tried to tend to my mother, but, of course, the whole country was in shock, and I knew this was an awful event. I had my mother on my mind. All of a sudden without her being there, life seemed very unstable. By the time Sunday rolled around I was at one of my father's brother's apartments, which was around the corner from the Mazzine household. They lived on the second floor, and while I was looking at their fish tank in the living room, the television, of course, was tuned into the Kennedy assassination. I remember my father and the other people there being shocked as we all watched Jack Ruby shoot Oswald. I saw it live as it was happening, and it seemed like the world was falling apart.

I tried to go along with whoever was taking care of me, but everyone was so sad and crying, especially Gramps. I started wondering if there was something terribly wrong with my mother, and maybe I would never see her again. Maybe they were hiding something from me. I couldn't tell whether the sadness was over President Kennedy or my mother, and I kept remembering her last words to me saying she had to live for her son. I never realized how much I loved and missed her. I started getting very frightened for the first time.

On November 25th they had the funeral for the president and, though I know most people remember little John saluting as the motorcade went by, the thing that stood out in my mind most, maybe because of my love of horses, was the beautiful black horse without a rider prancing up and down. It represented that someone was gone. In my eight-year-old mind, I felt like I was the horse and didn't have a mother. With the sadness going on in the country, I also remembered how happy my mother had been when she voted for the first time for President Kennedy. I felt like it was the end of the innocence.

My father assured me that my mother was going to be okay and would be home in a couple of days. On the day she was to arrive home, Gramps and I sat looking out the window waiting for the car to pull up. As she walked around the house to come in the door, I ran to her and we hugged like we had never hugged before. I was in total joy to see my mother after those dark days. She was home, she was alive, and she said to me, "1 told you I'd be back. I would never leave you like my mother left me. I told the doctor I couldn't die because I have Anthony at home." It was a wonderful feeling to think that my little life was going to get back to normal even though people were still mourning the death of our president.

Not only did my mother come home, but she brought something with her—a new fear, the fear of dying. This fear really took hold. I still don't understand the correlation of her being operated on the same day the president was assassinated, but somehow there was one. She came back from the hospital a hypochondriac. In her mind, she was going to die. She spent endless hours looking at herself with a hand-held mirror, searching for any aftereffect of the operation on her beautiful face. Lying in bed, she would look to see if her mouth pulled to one side. She felt twitching in her muscles. I assured her nothing was happening, but she believed her face was pulling to one side.

My role was to take care of her until she felt better. I now felt that I was the adult taking care of my sick child, and I really did love her as if she was my daughter. I would do anything that it took to make her well again. She quickly got used to me doing everything for her while she stayed in bed. My father was working two jobs at the time, so he wasn't home much. I now was cleaning the house, shopping, doing the laundry, and sometimes cooking with my mother's instructions. We moved a small black and white television set into my parents' bedroom and placed it on a stand so she could watch it in bed.

The country was still in shock over the death of the president and uncertainty lingered on through that winter. In my little world there was also a lot of uncertainty; I wondered if my mother was ever going to get better. Every night, when my father was working as a security guard at a hamburger joint, my mother and I would play board games—Scrabble, Clue, Monopoly, whatever she was in the mood for. This was actually comforting. By spending so much time with each other, my mother and I bonded like we had never done before or since. I would do whatever was necessary to keep her happy, going along with her every whim. For instance, in the evening, she would always want an ice cream sundae. But she always seemed to wait until the candy store on the corner was about to close. She would tell me she had a "desire," and I would run to get there right before they closed. By that time, the lady who owned the place had had one too many 'nips' and was tired and had just cleaned up all her utensils. She was grumpy, saying, "Why do you always wait 'til the last minute?"

I told her I was sorry, but my mother was sick in bed and I was just trying to keep her happy. Then, I'd get lucky. Her husband would come to my rescue and make the ice cream sundae for me. I knew it was a pain in the ass for him to start all over and use all the things they'd just cleaned, but he would do it anyway. Thank God.

One night, I got there, and the store was dark; the door was locked. I could see them through the window, but they weren't going to open up, so I went back home and told my mother there would be no ice cream that night. She blamed me for taking too long to get there. I felt terrible that I'd disappointed her; I was trying so hard. But, if one thing went wrong, she would act like a disappointed child, and I would feel like a father who had let his daughter down.

The winter nights of 1963 dragged on. Our regular routine of playing games made for many fun-filled nights. We were like two kids acting as if our parents went away and left us alone. Sometimes we'd have a surprise guest. It would be my father in his security guard outfit with a hat that was much too big for him. He had a little badge and a nightstick. He looked like Phil Silvers, an old-time actor who played Sergeant Bilko in a comedy series at the time. My mother would be worried that he had left his post at the burger and shake place. He was supposed to be watching a group of teenagers that loitered there and sometimes broke windows. My mother would ask who was watching the place while he was gone. My father, in his classic style, would say, "The kids are." He assured my mother that they were always good on his shift. They weren't bad kids and he got along with them fine. "You just have to know how to handle them. They only break the windows when the other guy is on shift."

We would open the paper bags he brought, and we'd all enjoy the hamburgers and fries inside. After about a half hour he'd say he had to go "back to the kids" and my mother and I would continue on with our board games.

My mother kept telling me that she lived because of me. This left a heavy burden on my mind. She hadn't mentioned for a long time the haunting words of how she could have aborted me or given me up for adoption and how she sacrificed her life for me. The new line

was, "1 stayed alive just for you." I was going to do everything in my power to deserve her "sacrifices." However, her fear of dying never left her. Thinking back to those months when we spent time together, I realized that this was probably the only time she had gotten any nurturing in her life and she enjoyed being in that role. Thank God, she rose from the bed by springtime because my mind was on baseball and the Mets and a new season of hope. This year was extra special because the Mets were getting their own new stadium in Flushing Meadows, Queens.

Of all the memories of that year, the one that stands out is my first time going to Shea Stadium. It was a night game. The San Francisco Giants were in town, and my father wanted to see his old team again. All the stars he remembered were returning to New York to play the Mets. Of course, he wanted to see Willy Mays, his favorite, who he considered the greatest ballplayer of all time and I have to agree with my father on that. He could do everything and make it look so easy. Going with my father to a ball game was a different experience than most kids have when they go to a game. First, when we would pull up to park, my father would show his city employee card and tell the gatekeeper that he was with the ground crew and we would just drive through without paying. Next, we never bought tickets for a game; he had an old neighborhood friend who worked there and arranged things. There was this door by the visitors' bullpen. At

a specific time, we would knock twice on the door. It would open, my father would shake hands with his old friend, and he would whistle up the hall to another man who would take us through the tunnel and to the seats. Next, that man would give us to another man who would show my father to box seats right behind the Giants' dugout. The man would politely wipe down the seats with his little rag, my father would hand him a dollar and say, "Thanks, Johnny."

My father called everyone Johnny if he didn't know his name; it's a lesson I learned that has served me well. We always had the best seats in the house. My father knew how to work the system. He had street smarts; I guess that came from the Mazzine influence. I learned fast how to play the game.

When you're nine years old and walk through the entrance and see the field at night for the first time, if you love baseball, you never forget it. It's like you're living two days in one; first, you already have the day you lived and now the lit-up stadium brings you a whole new day. It's pure magic. I still get goose bumps every time I go to a night game. At the time, Shea Stadium was modern and totally state of the art. It was the new showcase of how a stadium could be. Orange and blue symbols, which are the New York colors and then became the Mets colors, were posted around. My father always wanted to get there early so that we could see the ball players warm up on the sidelines. Back then, you could get very close to the players and

sometimes they would come over and talk to you or give autographs to the fans. I don't think it's like that anymore. Because we were early, I had the opportunity to wander over to the first base side where the Mets dugout was. Even though they didn't have any stars, they were my Mets and that was all that mattered. I'll never forget the sight of Mrs. Joan Payson, the owner of the Mets, and thank God for her, with her big, fancy, floppy hats, cheering on the team in her box seat right behind the dugout. New York was thrilled with her for bringing a National League team back to New York.

My one little problem was that my father only took me when the Giants were in town. Sometimes I'd get lucky if a neighbor happened to be going to a game and asked me to come along. Other than that, I had to be content watching or listening on my transistor radio to every game the Mets played. The more they lost, the more I loved them, for they were my team. I wasn't alone. It seemed like the whole city was also falling in love. No matter how awful they were on the field, like Casey Stengel, 'the old professor' would say, "They are the Amazing Mets!" That name took hold. Even though Casey Stengel was past his prime, they needed a funny personality like his because he was a great promoter. Who cared about the Yankees with all their stars always winning? We were still able to outdraw them in attendance, for we were the new breed. Someday, we would put it all together and shine. We just had to keep waiting for our moment to arrive.

By now, I had fully converted my gramps into being a Mets fan. Of course, he still loved his memories of his Brooklyn Dodgers, or "Bums" as he would call them, but I think because of his love for me, he now was an ally of the new breed. He would never forget Jackie Robinson, Roy Campanella, Duke Snyder, and the rest of the clan. But remember, Gramps had come back to life when I was born, so he was going all the way with loyalty to me and the Mets. He had such patience to watch or listen with me through every game the Mets lost.

An interesting thing happened on Father's Day. Gramps came over so we could celebrate the day with him and, of course, the Mets were on. It was an unusually hot June day. We were having a little barbecue in the backyard, but, of course, as soon as game time came, I went in to watch it in the living room. Gramps followed me in, my loyal companion. Jim Bunning, the great Philadelphia pitcher, was on the mound that day. He was mowing the Mets down like I'd never seen. It was three up, three down, every inning. We couldn't get a hit; we couldn't even get a walk or reach first base on an error. As I watched, I still had faith that somehow we would at least get a hit, but Jim Bunning was unbelievable that day. By the seventh inning, he was working on a perfect game. By the eighth inning, I noticed Gramps was no longer hoping for the Mets to get a hit. The Mets were mowed down in the eighth inning and they were behind, as I remember, six-

nothing. By the ninth inning, Gramps is now rooting for Jim Bunning and with the first Met out, Gramps is getting ecstatic, and he tells me, "Two more to go, Champ, and he will have pitched a perfect game!"

If you know anything about baseball, this is probably the rarest feat to ever achieve. I think it had only happened two or three times in the history of baseball. The second Met up that inning, also was shut down by Jim Bunning. Jim Bunning needed one more out to complete this rarest occasion.

I turned to Gramps and said, "Who are you rooting for?"

He said, "Champ, we're not gonna win this one. It's Father's Day and he's one out away from pitching a perfect game. Let's let him have his day in the sun."

His whole family was there getting ready for him to get one more out, so that they could celebrate with him. When that last out was made, Jim Bunning had pitched a perfect game and Gramps started crying. Pitching the perfect game was so rare; it was the first time that this had happened in the National League since 1880. On that day I learned what sportsmanship and being a good loser was about. The Mets' fans in the stands also got up and gave him a standing ovation in support of his unbelievable effort. The lesson Gramps taught me that day has stayed with me for life. He said that it wasn't my day yet; my day would come, but today let it be Jim Bunning's day.

The Ties That Bind

We still visited the Mazzine house on Sundays. One day when I got out of the car, I was startled to see some of my uncles on the roof holding rifles. I asked my father what was going on. He told me they were looking for rats to keep them away from the prize carrier pigeons they made money on. He assured me that they were only BB guns.

In all the years of visiting the house, I'd never been upstairs. It seemed to be off limits, but I was getting curious about what I would see if I climbed the long dark wooden staircase. One day I asked my father if he'd show me the room that he slept in growing up. Much to my surprise, he said yes. As we walked up, the steps were very creaky, not from my little feet but from my father's. When we got to the landing, I realized there were no doors to any of the rooms. On the floor in my father's old room was a bare mattress, and there was no other furniture. The window was open, and a slight breeze was stirring the curtains. We stood looking out, and my father pointed to a roof on one of the buildings near the house that he would sleep on during hot summer nights to get away from all the noise.

Amazingly, from up there I could not hear a sound from anything going on downstairs in the dining room. It seemed to all disappear. I wanted so badly to walk down the hall because I was trying to figure out how my grandparents and eleven kids could possibly live here. I could tell that my father was a little embarrassed. It seemed like he had not been up there in years, so I didn't want to push it. Then he told me he had a secret. He went over to a little piece of floor paneling and picked up the wood and told me this was his hiding place. He said, "When you have nine brothers, you have to have a hiding place."

When he lifted it up, there were some old coins that he had left behind. He took them out and handed them to me, and I put them in my pocket. That started my interest in coin collecting. I couldn't believe all the years that had gone by and how many people must have walked over my father's hiding place without ever discovering it.

During this time, one of my uncles had gotten in way over his head gambling, and he owed the Shylock a lot of money, and they were looking for him. I was listening in, probably when I shouldn't have been, while the brothers talked about how they were going to take care of the situation. I don't know if it was Uncle Frank who took care of it or his brothers, but I know that my uncle disappeared for a while. They sent him to Florida, until things calmed down. Eventually he came back.

One of the most memorable events of life with the

Mazzines was when my father told me we were all going to have a family reunion, and at the same time, we would be visiting Uncle Sal in the hospital. All the cars met at the Mazzine household and, like a caravan, we all drove away for our journey. Everyone had packed lunches and refreshments. I was excited about this—all of us being at the same place at the same time and being with my cousins. As I sat in the back seat, I felt the ride getting longer than I thought it would be. The countryside was beautiful, far removed from where we came. After a couple of hours, my father said, "We're finally here."

All the cars in a line drove through a brick archway. Right in front of us were a bunch of picnic benches. This was going to be great. People started emptying their cars bringing food to the tables. My father told me that, being that we were at a hospital, only two could go in at a time, and, of course, no children were allowed. He assured us that when the adults went in, they would have Uncle Sal wave to us from the window joined by men waving from other windows as well. When my father came out from his visit, and we were about to have lunch, I mentioned that it didn't look like a hospital to me because when Uncle Sal waved to us, I noticed bars on the window and all the men were wearing the same kind of clothes.

I said, "I think this is a jail."

As my father spit out his sandwich, he picked me up like I was a feather and ran me off away from the rest of the gang. He bent down, pointed to me, and said,

"Anthony, you're the oldest of all the cousins here, and they think it's a hospital. Promise me, you don't mention jail again. I know you understand, but they don't."

I went back to the picnic bench and never said a word.

No matter what people thought of the Mazzines and their way of life—living on the edge of society, being rebels—they did have codes of behavior and they lived by three main ones. One was never to rob from someone who has less than you. Never steal from the Church. And third and most important, be loyal to family and friends and never be a "rat."

One sunny Sunday in the summer, I was sitting on the stoop with Queenie. Most of the brothers were in the backyard playing bocce ball. My grandfather was looking out the window at the dog and me, and suddenly, Queenie took off after a cat or something and ran straight into the street. It was not a well-travelled street, probably because people wanted to avoid the Mazzine house. At that moment, there was a car that might have been going a little too fast, perhaps because you never knew what could happen on that street. As Queenie dashed out, there was a screech of the wheels as she went under the car. Before I could even get up from the stoop, the Mazzine brothers came running out to see what had happened. The man got out of his car and started to explain that he couldn't help but hit her. By now, about five of the brothers had surrounded him and this man was trembling. I thought he was

going to catch a beating, but my father turned to me and asked, "Anthony, what happened?"

I told him that Queenie just ran straight out in front of the car and there was no way this man could have seen that. My father put his hand on the man's arm and said, "The kid said it wasn't your fault. There was nothing you could do."

The man was still shaking, but he was relieved, and the brothers even asked him if he wanted to come in the house to have a drink and calm down. He politely said no to that and got in his car and drove away, very slowly. The brothers picked up Queenie. They didn't want me to see her. I was told to stay on the stoop, and they brought Queenie into the backyard. Grandpa Mazzine just sat in his chair in silence. Sometimes, when my mother would argue with my father, she would push his buttons by putting down his family and telling me not to grow up like them. But, on that given day, I was proud to be a Mazzine.

The death of Queenie stayed with me for a long time. The Mazzine house just wasn't the same without her. Grandpa Mazzine became more reclusive than ever, hardly leaving his chair in the living room. He would spend his time just staring out the window. His cough was getting worse. Before Queenie died, he would get up and give me a fish to take home when I was ready to leave. Now, he did not move from his chair; instead, I would have to go over to him and kiss him goodbye.

Almost Suburbia

As usual, in 1964, the Mets came in last place again, but that was okay with me. They only lost 109 games; there was a little improvement, and they were still considered the worst team in baseball. But to me, there was always hope for next spring. The older players were retiring, and new younger players were starting to come up from the farm system. And, amazingly, even though they were the worst team in baseball, they drew 1,700,000 people to their new ballpark, Shea Stadium. This is unheard of in professional sports. They might have found every way in the world to lose, but they never lost the fans who loved them; we would stay loyal through thick and thin. We were willing to wait for our day in the sun.

My mother had gotten very used to all the extra work I did when she was recuperating from her ear operation. She leaned on me for things a nine-year-old didn't usually have to do. I just wanted to keep her happy, but now that I was older, I realized that I was constantly afraid that she could unleash horrible accusations. For example, if I made a face or acted like I didn't want to do something, her comeback was, "Don't you know because of you I can't have children? You ruined my insides, and this is the thanks I get." When you know that is coming, you do whatever you can not to hear those words. Of course, I could never tell my gramps because he would explode. Even though I was beaten down, I would go to the stores for her, do the laundry, and complete whatever tasks she might dole out. On the outside, I looked like a nice kid helping my wonderful mother. I didn't let anyone see how miserable I felt.

When I wasn't doing my mother's bidding, I did regular kid things like riding my bicycle through town, playing street games with other kids, and using baseball cards to clothespin between the spokes so that it sounded like a motorcycle. I would never use a New York Mets baseball card; I used Yankee cards because that was how I felt about them.

As the year was coming to an end, we got our first, brand new car. All past cars were "old bombs." My father was very proud to drive out of the showroom in a 1964 maroon Chevy Impala Super Sport with bucket seats. Maroon must have been the color of the year. It seemed like every new car was maroon. He loved the bucket seats; they must have been a new feature in cars because he never stopped talking about them. My father was always outside in the driveway cleaning the car. He was meticulous. He had worked hard and had such pride of ownership. I can still see our house with my father's brand-new car sitting in the driveway.

My parents had a great circle of friends and did

a lot of socializing. It seemed there was a party for every occasion. Everyone in our little four-block area knew one another, so most of their friends were the parents of the kids that I hung out with. Some of the people might have gotten babysitters for their kids, but I was so adult-like I never had a babysitter. Also, I had Gramps. My parents were living a happy lifestyle. They were still very comical. Before each party, my mother would lecture my father not to drink too much like his brothers and get silly and embarrass her. Every time she gave that speech, she would get drunk at the party. It didn't take much for her to get tipsy, but she would pay the price the next day with a hangover.

Out of all the parties, the most memorable were the Halloween parties. The neighbors would take turns throwing the various parties in their new hip, suburban place—the finished basement. Everyone had to wear a costume to the big event. There would be a prize for the best one. This particular year, my father had decided he would go dressed as a woman. I guess he got the idea from me since I went as a girl the year before. He was sitting in the kitchen in a tight blue dress, wearing heels, a jet-black wig, blue band in his hair, and fake breasts. My mother and her friend were putting makeup on him, including false eyelashes. My father had a big, crooked nose, so he could have been the ugliest woman that I've ever seen. But they did an unbelievable job making him up. My father was in good shape, and if you didn't look at his face, he didn't look bad.

Just as my mother was putting the finishing touches on his makeup, the doorbell rang. It was our neighbor telling us that some kids were trick-or-treating, and they took my father's little cement angel off his beloved birdbath on the front lawn. With my mother still holding the eyebrow pencil, my father leaped out of his chair, high heels and all, and ran out the door to chase the kids holding his cement cherub. Once he realized he really couldn't move in the high heels, he kicked off his shoes and, with the speed of the Mazzines, ran full tilt down the street. Just when he was about the catch the kids, they dropped his statue, and he stopped to pick up the pieces and brought it back home to us. He said, "Mary, I almost got those little bastards. They got away, but at least I got my little guy back. He's in two pieces, but I'll cement them back tomorrow."

My mother did the finishing touches on his makeup by giving him a beauty mark, and off to the party they went. Legend has it that when they arrived, a man was there who didn't realize it was my father dressed as a woman. This man, who had arrived half in the bag, turned to my uncle and said, "It's a shame this girl is such a beast. Look at the shape on her and what a set of tits."

My uncle said, "That's Pete."

The man replied, "I think I've had too much to drink"

Needless to say, my father won the Halloween prize.

The Holiday Season

With the first snowfall of the year, Miriam and I came up with an idea of how to make some extra money. We would go door to door and ask if people wanted us to shovel the paths in front of their houses. We would charge fifty cents so we each made a quarter. We woke up early in the morning, got dressed quickly, and put on our gloves, winter coats, and boots. My little tomboy friend always wore a scarf. Before we went out, my father told us we could not charge older women who lived alone. "Just do it for them."

We started on the corner and worked our way up the street. All the neighbors thought this was a great idea. No one said no to us. Even people we didn't ask for money would come to the door and insist they pay us. The older women living alone, especially, were insistent that not only they pay us but they offered us hot chocolate as well. However, we were on a mission and didn't want to break our momentum by stopping for refreshments. We were a great team. We planned to continue doing this every time it snowed. My father, who was very into the weather, would give us the forecast the night before. We had our system down to a science. Miriam was the best buddy a nine-year-old boy could have.

That year, as usual, my family spent Christmas Eve and Christmas day down the street at Aunt Jeanette's. Of course, Gramps would come along; the boys were also his grandchildren. Since I was past the age of believing in Santa Claus, I had fun watching my cousins waiting for him to arrive. When they would come down the stairs to open their presents, it was like a scene from a Norman Rockwell painting, that is, except for when Gramps would go through his annual crying episode about his wife Theresa not coming home for Christmas years ago. We all knew when that moment was coming. It was like on cue when he would hear the song, "I'll Be Home for Christmas." That would break him. Also, on cue, my mother would try to stop him from crying about "that tramp," her mother. I don't think she was trying to be mean. She was just trying to cover up the hurt she had inside. On a lighter note, my father would really get into the spirit and make believe he was Santa Claus, ringing a bell and shouting, "Ho, ho, ho." One year he was taken off guard when the kids were already down the steps. My cousin, Junior, saw my father and went to my mother and said, "Aunt Mary, I think Uncle Pete is nuts; he thinks he's Santa Claus!"

In fourth grade, once again I had a nice teacher, but I was getting used to just barely getting by in my grades. I started seeing a trend in their notes. They would write,

"Anthony is a very polite and well-mannered boy but has trouble concentrating on his work."

What they didn't know was that I was daydreaming about my secret life with Gramps, the Mazzines, and my New York Mets. While they were teaching, they had no idea how good I had become at figuring out New York Mets batting averages and ERAs of the pitchers. Some subjects interested me, and I did well in those, but in other subjects I was just somewhere else. I also noticed a trend where they would write. "He brings an interesting perspective on topics and very astute observations." My teachers were completely unaware of all the things I had already seen in my short life. How could I relate my life experiences to them? Even with Miriam, I would always hide my past. I felt she wouldn't understand. I just knew I had to continue on.

In February, I was already thinking about Spring training. As April would get closer, I'd be trying to figure out which players would make the team. I knew every Met player by the number on their jersey. I'd talk to Gramps about the kind of year the Mets might have. He thought the Mets were worse than his Brooklyn Bums, but he was a true believer. I wanted to be the best of the true believers, and I loved to hear Gramps and my father talk baseball. Although they loved different teams, they both agreed that the National League was better because they allowed blacks to play professional baseball before the American League did. They would

talk about how loyal they were to their teams before they had left for California. I wanted them to know that I was just as loyal to my New York Mets as they were to their teams, for we were the new breed. We were young, and we had our own dreams.

My little town of Rosedale was continuing to go through the Italian invasion. One of my mother's aunts moved across the street from Aunt Jeanette. That was okay with me, but then my mother's cousins moved right next door to us. I found this to be too confining. There were only about twelve feet separating the houses. The cousins were nice people; they had three kids, two boys around my age and, with them came Aunt Gracie, Gramps's sister.

I felt their proximity confining because when my parents fought, they'd be very loud and didn't hold back. Sometimes my father got close to hitting my mother, and, if I didn't step in, it might have happened. I did get pushed around several times. My mother never knew when to shut up. She would just push at my father's sensitive spots. The two incendiary topics were his family and money. When the fights began, I would run to close the windows even though I knew they could still probably hear everything. When I left the house, I would walk face down, not wanting to make eye contact. Sometimes when the arguing would happen and Miriam and I were close to the house, she would be kind enough to pretend that she didn't hear. After their bouts, my parents would go on as if nothing

had happened, but I felt ashamed of their behavior and did not recover quickly.

Although the fights were traumatic, most of the time the general atmosphere was like a party filled with fun and laughter, especially in the summer. We would take turns in whose backyard the parties would happen. The fearful old residents, who had been there since the land was made up of potato farms, were right. We were loud and the music was blaring. I especially enjoyed observing Gramps and his sister. She was still in shock about the change in him since I was born. My mother's family was quite different from the Mazzines, but both were entertaining in their own unique ways.

We Were Only Playing

New York winters could be unpredictable, but New Yorkers were very predictable. If they heard there was even a slight chance of snow, they would flock to the stores and buy everything in sight, emptying the shelves and creating a shortage that did not have to be. My father was more fanatical than most, even buying bags of rock salt to melt the snow if and when it came. Ninety percent of the time, no snow fell or there was just a slight dusting. More often than not, it was rain that fell. But, once overnight, a snowstorm came without any warning catching everyone off guard. It was more snow than I'd ever seen, and it was beautiful—a winter wonderland. Roads were undriveable. Not only were the cars snowed in, but the people were also snowed in. Everything came to a halt. It was a kid's dream but not much fun for people like my father.

After being snowed in for days, my father never wanted to be caught off-guard again. He went out and bought a snowblower. He now felt secure that if it ever happened again, he was ready, and he wanted everyone on the block to know about his new toy. After my father cleared our driveway, he went up and down the whole neighborhood clearing sidewalks and driveways making sure we had the cleanest block. He became the hero of the neighborhood. I was happy for him as he performed his civic duty. Unfortunately, he put Miriam's and my snow removal team out of business. Well, it was fun while it lasted. On the bright side, we got more time to play on what we called "snow days" when we didn't have to go to school because of a storm. We had a lot of fun, but suddenly it all came to an end.

Miriam's house was always in disrepair. They never took care of the lawn. They didn't fix things around the house; shingles would be broken and left that way. Her mother had four kids, and she was a very jolly, carefree woman who smiled at the world. I was invited in the house probably only twice in my life and had never seen anything like it. It almost made the Mazzine household look tidy. They were still wonderful people, and I never judged Miriam by the clutter and disarray of clothes all over the place, cats having kittens behind the couch, or open cans sitting on the kitchen table. Her father had a drinking problem; he could be a nice man, but he was often drunk. He owned a car repair garage and was a skilled mechanic when he was sober. The family always came out of the house dressed nicely. They were happy or at least seemed to be happy. Miriam was my friend and that was all that mattered. However, one day, when we were off from school because of a transit strike, Miriam and I and her brothers were playing one of our usual chasing games. I was running around the back

of the house when I reached their cyclone fence gate and barreled ahead. I assumed the gate would open when I pushed it, but it didn't; it was broken. Headfirst, I crashed into the top metal bar with my mouth and broke my two front teeth right in half. It stung for a second. There was no blood. I could see my two pieces of teeth on the ground and picked them up.

I calmly went into my house to tell my mother I had just broken my teeth thinking I was going to get some tender loving care, but instead, I got the beating of a lifetime. She started punching and hitting me, and I curled up into a ball on the floor. She was screaming and kicking. She said that they'd spent so much money on my teeth, and these were my permanent, adult teeth. Fortunately, her best friend, Ilene, who I called my Aunt Ilene, was there, and she was furious at how my mother was behaving; she pulled her off me. Then my father came home and both Ilene and my father were terribly upset at how my mother had handled the situation. It was totally uncalled for and totally unexpected. I had never been hit in my life, and my mother never did it again. I have no idea what came over her that day. My father told my mother to calm down; he would take me to the dentist.

This was the plan, but the next day, Miriam's father, Matt, came over and told my father he heard that I'd broken my teeth on their fence, and he had house insurance that covered things like that. My father refused saying we would take care of this on our own.

There was no sense in making a big deal about it, and he didn't really want to file a claim against them. Matt was adamant that this was how things were done; they owned houses, they were insured for this kind of thing, and this was what they paid insurance for. He insisted that my father must make a claim against the house insurance and that it would pay for my teeth, and he'd get a little money and that even if it came to a little more, I would have what was put into the account for after I was eighteen. My father, being unfamiliar with insurance companies, finally was talked into it. Matt brought over the paperwork with the insurance company's name and my father filed a claim, something totally against his nature to begin with.

A month or so later during the heaviest snowfall of the season, my father was in our driveway playing with the snow blower, and I was in my bedroom. I heard a commotion from outside; two men yelling. It was getting so loud that I could hear it through the storm windows. I peeked through the blinds and saw Miriam's father, who was drunk, yelling at my father accusing him of trying to take his house away and what kind of way was this for a neighbor to behave? My father was caught totally by surprise. I could hear him saying that he didn't want to file the claim in the first place and that he said he'd take care of his own kid's teeth. He didn't want their money or their house, but Matt would not let up, repeating over and over that we were trying to take their house away. My father,

who could be very tough, somehow restrained himself from punching him, but Miriam was there, pulling on her father's sleeve, trying to make him go back to the house. She was saying, "Dad, please stop!"

My father told her to take him home because he was drunk. It was very disturbing to see Miriam in such an embarrassing situation. My first instinct was to run outside and help calm things down somehow, but then I thought maybe it was better if Miriam didn't know I'd seen all this; my interfering might make it worse for her. I just stood there with my heart sinking for her, peeking through the blinds, praying that this would soon end. I hoped Matt would leave it alone before my father hit him. My father just left the snow blower where it was and came into the house. Miriam dragged her father back to their house.

After that, Miriam and I were never the same. Our wonderful friendship was over. We didn't know how to handle the situation, so we just avoided one another. I would try not to bump into Miriam knowing how embarrassed she must have been. The most we acknowledged was with a wave, but we never spoke again. I hurt for a long time not having Miriam as my buddy, and I'm sure she did too. Sometimes I think of the days when we were the two chimps, Jocko and Candy, running away from her brother, the hunter. I think of the note we wrote and put in a bottle and buried behind the garage, hoping that someday somebody would find it and know we were there. I wonder if

124

Miriam ever thinks about the wonderful times we had in those early years. She was my first real friend. Even now, as an adult, I still feel like there's a little piece of me in that bottle behind the garage.

Summer's End

Traditionally in New York, Labor Day is considered the end of summer. In Rosedale, families from the neighborhood would all gather at Brookville Park to celebrate with a big barbecue and events for the kids. That summer of 1965, as people were just settling in to have fun, it started to rain. Little by little, one by one, the people started congregating in our backyard, and the size of the group just kept growing. Neighbors helped my father carry the whole stereo console into our backyard. We had an awning to protect some of the people, but by the time everyone was gathered, it had stopped raining. The music played well into the night. It was one of the wildest, spontaneous gatherings of my childhood.

Kids, me included, were dancing the twist; everybody brought food and plenty of beer and soda to go around. The adults were really letting their hair down and dancing the limbo rock. We kids laughed hysterically watching the old people (who probably were in their thirties or forties) trying to bend lower and lower backwards to get under the limbo stick. The moments of the day lingered in my memory long after that night came to an end.

When it was over, it hit me. I was going to a new school—a Catholic school, St. Pius the 10th. It was a little parish with a modest church that looked like a rectangle built with simple cinder blocks. It didn't have all the ornate statues and ornaments and facades that you would ordinarily see. They had just completed a new, modern school shaped in a circle, something unusual. The only comfort was that it looked a lot like Shea Stadium. The school would start with grades one to five and continue to six, seven, and eight as the years went on. I was going into the fifth grade which meant that when I got to eighth grade, mine would be the first graduating class. My parents thought the regimen with stricter teachers—nuns—would encourage me to take learning more seriously, and the nuns probably wouldn't tolerate my daydreaming. I had promised my parents that I was going to try very hard to do better in school. This was a financial sacrifice for them. The pressure was on.

The teaching nuns were in the order of the Sacred Heart of Mary. They wore navy blue habits covering them from head to toe. The piece of material concealing their chests made it impossible to see any actual shape of the woman standing in front of you. A starched white rim around their faces covered their hair and ears. They all had rosary beads with Jesus on the cross hanging down. Their arms were fully covered. They wore black laced shoes. All you could see of the person under the habit was her face and hands.

The school had three floors, and the rooms were shaped like pie wedges. There were no windows to stare out of. In the middle of the three floors was an area used as an auditorium or for meetings, musical programs, and eventually, gymnastics. Not having windows was bad for me, a kid who liked daydreaming about freedom, baseball, and Gramps. Two large panes on each side of the back of the room, not facing us, provided the only glass in the room.

The Catholic Church was going through a transition at that time after Vatican Two. The Church was attempting to keep up with the modern era. For instance, these nuns did not hit children, and now Mass was said in English instead of Latin. This made sense because we never knew what we were saying in Latin; we just went through the motions. It was no longer a sin to eat meat on Friday. Many good Catholics found the changes difficult. My mother continued to send me to the German deli around the corner to buy cod fish cakes every Friday. I also think that not having to wear a school uniform was a result of the changes in the church. They knew times were changing and they didn't want to lose any faithful "Christian soldiers." There were even what they called "Folk Masses" with people playing the guitar and singing.

Cousin John's teacher in first grade, Sister Carmel Marie, was also in charge of the music curriculum for the school. She had a beautiful voice. She was trying to get a choir going and we were singing several unfamiliar

songs in church. It's possible that she had written these songs. They were actually quite good. Two stand out in my mind to this day. One was called "It's a Long Road to Freedom" and the other was "What Color is God's Skin?" I still remember the words:

What color is God's skin?
Is it black, brown or yellow? Red? Is it white?
Everyone's the same in the Good Lord's sight.

I think these words got under the skin of a lot of good, white, Christian people in our Rosedale community that was 99.9 percent white. Rosedale, after the Italians moved in, had gone about as far as the people wanted to go. To many people, Italians were the bottom of the barrel. The Italians then were starting to think they had "made it" and wanted to be the last ones included in this little, white enclave of New York City. It's funny how things change once you think you've made it.

I was off to a pretty good start in school. Because I was now going to Catholic school, my mother started taking me to church on Sundays. One thing that I did not like was going to confession. At the time, you couldn't receive Communion if you didn't go to confession, which meant that you had to tell the priest all your sins. Then the priest would assign a penance, such as saying a certain number of prayers—'Hail Marys' and 'Our Fathers.' The kids would stand in line in front of three or four confessionals—box-

like structures divided into three sections, the outer two behind black cloth, with the priest sitting in the middle behind an actual door. One "sinner" in the outer structure would confess while another would wait until the sliding grate on his side was pulled back by the priest so that he could confess through a screen. From the outside, you couldn't see which priest was in which confessional; you might be able to tell by his voice if you could hear it. I was always trying to figure which priest was easy and wouldn't give me a hard sentence. If I thought I was going to land with the tough priest, I'd back up a space and let another kid go before me. I didn't think I really had any sins, and I would made up a lot of stuff. I would say that I disobeyed my mother or cursed twice. It was totally ridiculous making up sins that I didn't feel I committed.

Communion is the most important part of the ceremony of the Mass; it symbolizes Jesus's Last Supper when Jesus told the apostles to "Drink this wine, it is my blood; eat this bread for it is my body." So, when a person receives the wafer representing the bread—something like a cracker—and drinks the wine from the chalice the priest offers, they have symbolically received Christ into their body. We were supposed to remember that Jesus died for our sins. You could only receive Communion if there was no *mortal* (very serious) sin on your soul that you hadn't confessed and done penance for.

Getting back to what mattered to me. The Mets

finished that summer in last place again, but amazingly drew huge crowds. Before 1965 ended, on November 9th, New York and the whole east coast experienced the biggest electrical blackout in history. It just happened to be my gramps's fiftieth birthday. He always used to say he thought he went blind that night. He was renting a room in a boarding house from a lady named Mrs. Kerns. He made it to our house, taking mass transit, and we all celebrated his birthday by candlelight. He slept over that night. I think it became his most memorable birthday. Two days before, he had bought me two beautiful, fancy black mollies, and since the fish tank was in the basement and the heater for the tank ran on electricity, I was so worried about my new pair of fish freezing to death that I wrapped the fish tank in towels, trying to keep the warmth in the water. When the lights came back on, the fish were alive.

The Duck

My father and I continued to visit the Mazzine house every Sunday. He was proud of the way I behaved, unlike the children of his siblings. My mother, distancing herself from that branch of the family, seldom came with us. However, she couldn't deny my father taking me there a couple of hours a week, since I spent most of my time with her father, although she made sure to upset my father before we left by saying I wasn't allowed to eat anything in that house, especially if my grandmother cooked it. (I did not eat there but took food away and told my grandmother I'd eat it when I got home. At home, my mother immediately made me throw it out.) With her first comment, she had already put the knife in my father but wanted to twist it one more time by saying, "They're nice people. They mean well, but when it comes to food you never know what you're going to get there," and then would come her refrain, "When I was dating your father, they invited me for a chicken dinner, and when I finished eating, they told me that I had just eaten the pigeons from the roof that couldn't fly anymore."

Nothing hurt him more than when she would say horrible things about the Mazzines. Even though he was not happy about the direction he saw his family going in, he didn't want to hear it from her. No matter what kind of lifestyle they would live, it was his family, his tribe.

One Sunday several weeks after Easter, my father said that we had to make a house call before going to the Mazzines. Apparently, the people we were going to see had gotten their daughter a duck for Easter, and now they didn't know what to with it. A lot of parents bought their children animals such as ducklings and bunnies and chicks for Easter thinking it was cute, but soon discovered the difficulties involved in caring for animals in an apartment. In this case, the duck, living in a cardboard box lined with newspapers, was growing. The novelty had worn off. Apparently, these people had made a phone call to my father for help, knowing that all unwanted animals were welcome at the Mazzine house.

The daughter, approximately my age, had grown attached to this little duck. She kept asking me whether it would be okay where we were taking it. I promised that her little duck was going to the greatest place an animal could live. I told her my grandfather Mazzine had such a way with animals and the love, care, and freedom this duck was going to get was beyond any other place. In my mind, I was thinking Grandpa Mazzine had never been the same since his dog, Queenie, had died and the house felt empty. I was excited about this because I thought the duck would bring Grandpa Mazzine happiness in some little way. My father saw my enthusiasm and let me run with it. I felt like an adult carrying the cardboard box and placing it securely in the back seat of the car.

At the Mazzine house, I asked my father if I could bring the duck in and give him to my grandfather Mazzine. As I walked down the long dark hallway, I felt like I was on a mission. I passed by the usual party in my grandmother's dining room and ran straight over to Grandpa Mazzine, sitting in his usual chair. And then it happened! I showed him what I had brought him, and his eyes lit up. It was love at first sight. I hadn't seen him smile in a long time. He wasn't even embarrassed to show that he had only a couple of teeth left. He picked up the little duckling and went straight out into the yard. He held it over his head with his two hands and started talking to it. I couldn't believe that this little surprise gift seemed to awaken him. He was so consumed with the duck that when my father and I went back into the house, he never came in. We must have been there for an hour and a half, talking to my uncles and grandmother who were all hanging out. When it was time to leave, we had to actually go back outside to say goodbye to him. I hugged him and he hugged me back like never before. This was a man who showed little emotion. He usually didn't talk to me much, but on that day, he was very animated.

On the ride home, my father and I were much more talkative than usual. My mother had tried to put up a wall between us, but I felt even closer to my father because of this event.

After that, every Sunday when we went to visit, Grandpa Mazzine was not in the house but sitting on the stoop with the duck. If he wasn't on the stoop with the duck, he was in the backyard talking to him. Each week, I was stunned by the progress of their relationship. It seemed like the duck was growing to be an adult so quickly and as it matured, the tricks that my grandfather taught it were amazing. This duck was doing things that I didn't even know were possible. For example, before long, the duck would follow my grandfather wherever he went and, on command, would stop when my grandfather told him to. Then, he got the duck to follow him to a certain place, like the candy store on the corner, and he'd tell it to wait outside for him. My grandfather would go in and come out and the duck would still be standing there waiting for him. Can you imagine walking down the street in Brooklyn and seeing a duck standing outside a store? They would walk across the street together. My grandfather could tell the duck to go ahead of him and come back on command. He seemed to have come alive. He was no longer a recluse in his chair. Grandpa Mazzine was now tending to his grapes in the small vineyard and making strong wine like he did in years past, and the duck was always with him.

The house was once a neighborhood attraction because of the goldfish pond, but now the duck took its place. People from the neighborhood came just to see the interaction of Grandpa Mazzine and his duck. Every Sunday, he would tell us the new things he had taught him, and when we were about to leave, he told us to thank the people who had sent him this gift and made us promise to tell the little girl that the duck was having a good life and so was he.

For years, every time I was in the girl's company, she would ask how her duck was doing, and I would tell her that she had no idea what she had done for my grandpa Mazzine. The duck never saw the inside of a cardboard box again.

I'll Do Better Next Year

My first year at St. Pius was more difficult than I could have imagined. The schoolwork proved to be much more challenging than public school. I thought I'd float by with manners and charm, but that didn't work with the nuns. They wanted me to study and do my homework, which, for me, meant opening up books on baseball. Even though there were no windows, I still managed to daydream and work out baseball statistics, which I had become quite adept at. My report cards were abysmal and severely disappointing to my parents; there was even a chance that I wouldn't get promoted. But I got through by the skin of my teeth. My parents, yet again, extracted another promise from me that I would do better next year.

After making that promise, I spent the whole summer listening to and watching every New York Mets game that I could. My parents were so upset by how badly I had performed that they put restrictions on me. Those restrictions robbed me of most of my fun that summer. I can only think of one highlight, and that was the annual Grandpa Mazzine Fourth of July birthday bash. Even though my mother was coming to the Mazzine house less and less, the Fourth was the one day she had to make an appearance. She had no use for my father's family, but there was a lot of warmth between her and Grandpa Mazzine. A month or so before the Fourth of July one of my father's brothers would drive to a southern state where fireworks were legal and load up. When he got back to New York, he made a lot of money selling every imaginable type of explosive, from cracker balls to roman candles, which were illegal in New York. By the time Grandpa Mazzine's birthday rolled around, the city of New York was ready and loaded to celebrate.

It was interesting how the system of policing worked in Brooklyn. We would watch the patrol cars go up and down the streets confiscating simple sparklers and simple firecrackers from kids in the neighborhood, but when they drove by the Mazzine household where there were flares, M80s, cherry bombs, and roman candles that were set off continually throughout the whole day, the police would just wave as they passed the house; they knew it was the annual Mazzine birthday. This was Mazzine's day and everyone in the neighborhood knew it. Friends, neighbors, and distant relatives would stop by to pay their respects. It was the happiest I'd ever seen my grandfather; he was being recognized and was the toast of the town, and right next to him was his new friend, the duck.

As summer came to an end, of course, My Mets had another losing year with a record of sixty-six wins

and ninety-five losses, but I was as enthusiastic as ever, and there must have been other people like me because they drew an attendance of almost 2,000,000. At school, there was also some hope on the horizon; I liked my new homeroom teacher, Sister Patrice, very much. She was young with beautiful blue eyes and considered very pretty. So pretty that my mother, after meeting her at a parent teacher conference, told me that she couldn't believe she was a nun because she was so good looking. As if you only become a nun if you were ugly. That was my mother's Elizabeth Taylor-fascination with looks. Sister Patrice could be very funny and always seemed bubbly. One day, she announced to the class that she thought she could liven up the room with a pet, but she made it clear that it would have to be an easy pet and asked if anyone had any recommendations. I raised my hand and said, "What about fish?"

She asked if I knew anything about taking care of fish. Of course, I told her I did. She announced to the class, "Anthony Albano will be in charge of our pet." Within two days, I brought in a fish tank and the accessories and one new pet fish. I took care of this tank religiously, and Sister Patrice and I were off to a good start.

As the year was coming to a close, I noticed that there was less fighting in my house between my mother and father. I hadn't even heard the haunting words of, "You ruined my insides, and I can't have children because of you," for several months. There seemed to be

something going on, but I couldn't figure it out. There were whispers between adults, but the conversations would stop whenever I came around. As I tried to put my finger on what was happening, I started to imagine things. When my father brought my mother to the doctor twice in a month, I thought maybe this was a recurrence of her previous illness. I was thinking that I didn't want to go through caring for her during the convalescent period again. But then I squashed that theory because they didn't seem unhappy, and when my mother and her sister got together whatever they were whispering about did not seem serious. They almost seemed happy. I could not put the pieces of this puzzle together.

Once during the holidays, when I was driving to the Mazzines with my father, I heard something on the car radio so raw and amazing that I was stunned. The man singing the song didn't have a good voice, but his words and the music were expressing all the pain I felt inside. I didn't even know you could say those kinds of things on the radio. I had never heard such anger, openness, and honesty before. The line that stood out for me was, "You shouldn't let the jugglers and the clowns do tricks for you." At that moment I thought I was the only person that ever felt that way. It brought me straight back to how I felt when my parents would take me to the circus. I thought how sad it was to make other people degrade themselves to make you laugh. I couldn't understand people's cruelty toward one

another, and someone was singing exactly about that. While I was absorbing every word, my body felt a wave of empowerment that I'd never felt before. The song was "Like a Rolling Stone" by Bob Dylan.

When the song ended, my father turned to me and said, "How do they let people like that on the radio. That was awful. Whoever is singing couldn't shine Perry Como's shoes." He turned the channel and when he got to something he liked he said, "Now this is music!" I was quiet. I didn't want to express the impact the song had on me. I filed that moment away in my head. I would catch up to this guy, Bob Dylan, down the road on my own.

At the Mazzines, still stunned by what I'd heard, I had to switch gears and get into the Christmas spirit. Of course, I went straight to Grandpa Mazzine and sat next to him in his chair. The duck was close by. He seemed happy again and was listening to the radio like in the old days. When the music on the radio stopped for the news, there was a report about the war in Viet Nam. They said there was going to be a truce in the fighting for two or three days over the Christmas holiday. This struck me as being so odd that I turned to my grandfather and said, "If people can stop fighting for a couple of days, why couldn't they just stop fighting?"

He put his arm around me, leaned over, kissed me, and said, "You are the most special kid I've ever seen. That's why I love you." I can still feel the bristles of his beard on my face.

The Shock

Still baffled by the truce in Viet Nam, I was witnessing a much more baffling truce right in my own house. Where did all the fighting go between my mother and father? It had been months since I last heard them arguing and having terrible words fly between them. They actually seemed happy. Yet, something else was going on. The whispers were getting more and more frequent and a little louder. There was actually a quiet jubilation going on around me. There were numerous private talks between my mother and Aunt Jeanette. I had never seen the two sisters as close as they were in the opening months of 1967. Whenever I walked in while they were talking, everything either got silent, or it was obvious that they had changed the subject. Thinking of it now, my mother was actually treating me nicely with no harsh, tormenting words in months. The mysteriousness of all these factors let my mind run away. I thought of all the possibilities.

The one I didn't put on my list that would catch me and our large circle of family and friends off guard was about to be revealed one day when they returned from yet another doctor's appointment. My father had said that they would have some news for me when they came home. I thought for sure my mother had some rare illness or her tumor in her ear had come back and also entertained many other theories. When they arrived home, we all sat down at the kitchen table. My mother put on her famous Elizabeth Taylor-smile, and my father asked how I would feel about having a baby brother or sister. "Your mother is pregnant."

I was shocked, but I didn't show any emotion. I said, "That would be nice; I think it's a good thing."

With both of them sitting there stunned, I got up and went into my room and closed the door. Alone, I fell to my knees and said, "Thank you, God. My prayers have been answered."

Jubilant is putting it mildly about how I felt. I was now free—free from guilt, free from having her tell me how I ruined her insides, free from hearing how she couldn't have children because of me. There was a baby coming. I'm twelve and free of all the attention always being on me. Now their focus would be on the little brat that was coming. This would be great. More time with Gramps. More uninterrupted time listening to and watching my Mets. I would be a teenager soon and free to do whatever I wanted, and no one would notice.

They were concerned about how I was going to react to having a sibling after being an only child. They thought maybe I'd be jealous of a new family member and that I would act out just to get attention. I learned afterwards that they kept it to themselves so long because they wanted to be sure, after all these years, that she was really pregnant. The news spread like wildfire around us. The comment that bothered me the most when my mother would be congratulated was that she would say, "Who would believe this? I thought I couldn't have any children." It infuriated me that these people didn't hear the words that I had heard throughout my life—about me ruining my mother's insides, making it impossible for her to get pregnant again. That was an image I had carried around and kept inside even from my father and Gramps.

I didn't know that this would be the longest pregnancy on record. The baby was due in late June. My parents were going through the usual motions—the crib was ordered, toys were bought, showers were given, and gifts received. There were months of celebration with Aunt Jeanette being the happiest. She and Uncle Funzi would be the godparents. When we broke the news to Gramps, he said he was happy but seemed unenthusiastic. He didn't care about any new baby as long as he and I were still a team.

My freedom didn't come immediately. On the contrary, I was disappointed to find that much more was expected of me. My mother excluded herself from any strenuous activity, including going food shopping, doing the laundry, and cleaning the house. These chores were left to me. I figured this was no time to rock the boat. All I had to do was get through it and wait until June.

There was a feeling in the air that things were changing, musically and politically. The summer of love was on its way.

The New Kid

I was missing my friendship with Miriam and felt a little lost without the closeness of one good friend. Yeah, the boys up the street that I played ball with were fun and we had some good times, but I wouldn't really say there was closeness. Then, as fate would have it, a new family moved in just up the block and they had five boys. I looked forward to meeting them and hoped they might be athletic and join in sports with us.

One of the five boys was exactly my age and would be going to my school. His name was Ed Kowalczyk, and we became good friends, but neither he nor his brothers were athletic. I always thought that Miriam was the best girl athlete that I'd ever seen, and Ed had to be the worst boy athlete I'd ever seen. I tried to include him in the stickball and baseball games that we played, but it wasn't for him. I was no super star by any means, only a mediocre ball player, but Ed had no coordination at all. He was very shy; I almost had to pull the words out of him. He was much more studious in school than me and was placed in the smarter group of kids. The classes were divided into three groups—advanced, regular, and whatever you want to call the one

I was in. We did find, however, that we had something in common—a fascination with coin collecting. When we walked to school together, our talks always revolved around coins. Once I got him going, we were on a crusade with our hobby, although he never understood my fascination with the New York Mets. To be honest, I don't know how he hung in there as my friend while I was always listening to or watching a Mets game.

Ed and I made an interesting duo. He was tall and lanky and, from a young age had to wear thick glasses just like the rest of his brothers. I was short and fit just like my father's side of the family, the Mazzines. We must have looked like Mutt and Jeff, Ed looking bookish and me looking athletic, but somehow we clicked. Once we were out of school, Ed and I would spend our days hunting for coins. Sometimes we'd get a ten-dollar bill, and, with it, we'd go into the bank on the corner, and ask for a roll of dimes or a roll of quarters. Then we'd go outside, check if we'd gotten lucky with any silver coins and then bring them back and continue this, sometimes for several hours, until the teller would have had enough of us and say that was it for the day. Sometimes Ed and I would trade coins, not only between us but with some of the adults who owned stores on the corner.

When Ed and I walked to school together there were usually two or three other boys with us. I know how peer pressure can be on kids, but there were just some things that Ed would join in that I disagreed

with. For a while, they all decided it would be fun to knock over all the empty garbage cans when they came home from school. Because I had so many more responsibilities at home than Ed and the boys, I didn't really think this was funny. I actually thought it was quite dumb. Back in our little neighborhood, news would spread quickly and before we knew it, neighbors had called the school. We were all reprimanded, even though I did not partake in this activity. I guess it was guilt by association.

Another thing that really disturbed me was that every day we had to pass a house and in the yard, there would be a retarded man sitting. Ed and the boys would relentlessly tease and taunt him, and he would get terribly upset. I told them that they shouldn't be doing this, and didn't they have any empathy for the poor soul? But they wouldn't pay attention to me. I even tried to persuade them to walk to and from school up a different block so that we didn't have to pass that house. Of course, I never told them of all the pain and suffering I had seen in my short life in my own family.

One day the man's sister came running out of the house very upset. She started yelling at us, asking why we teased her brother every day and couldn't we see he wasn't well? She was wearing a house dress with a big winter coat on. The other boys ran, but I just stood there. While they were well out of sight, she grabbed a hold of me and asked how we kids could be so cruel. I tried to explain to her that I'd told them not to tease her

brother, but they wouldn't listen. She was so upset that she started shaking me, saying I was one of those boys and she saw this every day. I told her I would never do this to her brother. I had a cousin who was a dwarf, and I had a retarded uncle, and I was so sorry for what they had done to her brother. She began to cry and wrapped her winter coat around me and said, "You poor child. I am so sorry."

A Ball of Confusion

While most kids were getting ready for summer fun, I didn't have any idea of what was in store for me. My father, ecstatic, woke me up on the morning of June 27, 1967, with the news that I had a sister named Maria. He asked me how I felt about that, and I told him that I wished I had a baby brother, but this would have to do.

It's interesting how life happens. Aunt Jeanette had tried so hard to have a girl, but Uncle Funzi had "cut her off" after five boys. My mother, who got pregnant after twelve years of trying, was the one to have a girl. Aunt Jeanette, however, was delighted with the new addition to the family and vowed to be the best godmother she could. She was going to do all the things with my sister that she couldn't do with her boys like buy her dresses and dolls. As she held my sister in her arms, Aunt Jeanette said something sincere to my mother about how nice it would have been if their mother had been there to see her first granddaughter. Gramps and I sat there as my mother shot back, "Oh, how could you even think of that bitch? I hope she's dead!"

Gramps said, "Mary, how can you even speak like that? She's still your mother."

My mother said, "Oh, please! She's nothing but a tramp, no matter who she is!"

Then there was silence.

All neighborhood news filtered through the Mazzine house and my father had heard about sightings of my long-lost grandmother, Theresa. Aunt Jeanette and Gramps were always pleading to my father for more news of my grandmother and her whereabouts. We heard that she was living in Ohio and had visited New York. My mother forbade my father from talking about her. I don't know how much my father knew about Theresa, but whenever Aunt Jeanette could get him cornered, she would pump him for information if my mother wasn't around.

My parents wanted Gramps and me to be enthusiastic about the baby. They put her into Gramps's arms, but he didn't seem comfortable or interested. Then it was my turn. I tried to hold her with care. They taught me to hold the baby's head up all the time. I didn't know they were prepping me to be the new babysitter. My mother tried to get Gramps enthused by telling him that he should remember when he used to hold me like this, but it didn't work. He just nodded and said he remembered, but he handed the baby back to my mother right away.

I noticed that things were beginning to change with Gramps. He started to get paranoid, worrying about

me all the time. Whenever I went out, he wanted to know who I was going with, when I'd be back, and why I didn't stay home with him. I felt bad but wanted to do things that twelve-year-olds do, like going on coin hunts with Ed or record hunting at Sam Goody's Music Store in Greenacres Mall. I could spend hours looking at different albums. When I was home, Gramps would be so disappointed that I'd left him. I was very torn.

When Easter rolled around, Aunt Jeanette hosted a festive gathering with all the relatives, and, out of the clear blue, Gramps started crying and talking as if his wife had just left him. His mind was transported back to those awful days, and it sounded like he was speaking gibberish. At that point, all the older relatives started speaking in Italian; they never spoke Italian in front of us unless they were cursing or it was serious and something kids shouldn't know. I wanted to hold him, but the adults made me go to the backyard to play with the other kids. Frightened that I was losing my gramps, I tried to listen at the door. I pleaded with my father to let me in. I wanted to tell Gramps that I would never leave him, and we'd always be together. I told my father that I was the only one who could get through to him, that he would listen to me, but it was to no avail.

Gramps was never the same. He fell back into the deep depression he'd been in before I was born. They didn't let me see him until he had been placed in a mental institution in Oyster Bay, Long Island. It was about an hour's drive from where we lived, and my father and sometimes my mother would take me to visit him. I'd wait on a picnic bench outside the place until they brought him out to see me. I think they didn't want me to see the inside. He'd come out but didn't possess any of the energy he had in his prime or the same excitement about seeing me. He was only fifty-seven. I know they were trying different medications on him to help with his paranoia. One of them made him very thirsty, and he would constantly move his mouth up and down. I tried to talk to him about the Mets and our time together, but he wouldn't be in the mood for chit chat. It seemed like he couldn't wait to get back inside where he felt safe. I don't know if this was possible or in his imagination, but he told me he had a girlfriend in there. My father brought me there as often as he could; he was very good about letting me stay connected to Gramps.

Dancing in the Streets

I was a little too young to be part of the summer of love in 1967, but I certainly felt the spirit in the air. The music on the radio was also changing; the themes were about peace, flower power, and ending the war in Viet Nam, a new kind of world coming. My best friend and sidekick, Ed, brought over record albums his older brothers listened to. I was introduced to people like Bob Dylan, Phil Ochs, and other folk singers. I especially loved the protest songs. These albums slowly replaced my collection of 45s. My first musical influence was Johnny Cash. When I heard his voice, I knew he felt my pain. I ordered his album on the Sun record label from television on my own. I never cared about a pretty voice. I was after what these songwriters had to say. This started my obsession with singer-songwriters.

Although my mind was becoming enlightened by the music I listened to, I kept my opinions to myself. I had no time for dancing in the streets; I was just trying to keep up with all the things I had to do. After being an only child for twelve years, I had a baby sister, and my mother needed more help. She bought me a Timex watch to keep track of time while I did all her errands. I did everything she asked to keep her happy and to prevent any verbal attacks. A lot of people in my neighborhood thought I was a good kid; I put on a happy face but was still tormented inside without Gramps. Ed was a good sport; he always went with me when I shopped for my mother. I had to ask them to put it in the book until my father got paid. Ed eased my embarrassment by pretending he wasn't paying attention.

Right before summer was ending, Ed and I went into a store called Bambi's Stationery after its owner, Al Bambus, and we asked if we could work there. We had learned that his two young workers were leaving for college. He immediately said yes. Now, Ed and I really felt adult. We had jobs! Twenty hours each a week, one dollar an hour. The reason I was so into working was because I hated when my mother and father would fight about money. She would always belittle him in front of me saying he didn't make enough money. The poor guy was working two jobs, and I thought my $80 a month would relieve some of the pressure.

Even though Miriam and I didn't talk anymore, I noticed that she was growing up to be a lovely young lady. It made me sad that we didn't have our friendship. The Mets finished in last place again, but they were my team, win or lose. It looked like they had a real star pitcher in a young man named Tom Seaver, who unbelievably won sixteen games playing for the worst team in baseball. And according to the Mets official

Tidewater Report, which was their farm team, they had a lot of great players coming up. Also, after the season, there was talk that when baseball began the next year, the Mets would be getting a new manager.

Luckily for me, I got Sister Patrice for my homeroom teacher again. She was fun, lovely, and a little quirky and went easy on me since I was a poor student. Yes, there was a God.

Bambi's

B ambi left it up to Ed and me to decide who would
work what hours, and I soon realized that even
though Ed and Bambi were both Polish, Bambi liked
me better. It was wonderful. He always had music
playing in the store, mostly his favorite old-fashioned
tunes. He used to call me his little guinea as I was
Italian. Back then, you didn't have to be politically
correct, and you could say that kind of thing. I didn't
mind because it was his way of showing affection.

Bambi taught me a lot about business. As each
month went by, he started to give me more responsibility.
I was put in charge of overseeing the delivery of toys
and board games, and I put the price on items. I would
write the price down, then slash it and write another
lower price below it that always ended in a nine. If
it were $2.00, I had to slash that number and make
it a $1.89 so that the customers thought they were
getting a bargain. He also taught me that when you're
in business, you should never have a political point
of view. I learned that right before the 1968 election
between Nixon and Humphrey. A man came in talking
politics to Bambi, and he was pretty riled up; he told

Bambi that we had to get Nixon in, and Bambi said, "You're absolutely right; we gotta get Nixon in." Ten minutes later another man came in all riled up and said that we had to get Humphrey in, and Bambi said, "You're absolutely right; we have to get Humphrey in."

I was restocking the candy and couldn't believe what I had just heard. So, when no customers were in the store, I said, "Bambi, I don't understand; you told one man, Nixon and one man, Humphrey."

He turned to me seriously and said, "Anthony, in business the customer is always right; you just agree." He also said, "I'll teach you everything I know, and it'll take five minutes." That always stayed with me. He was very kind to me. Even though he would rather have listened to music on the radio, he would let me listen to the Mets games, and he would forever say, "I don't why you're interested in the worst team in baseball."

I did have one big responsibility that was extremely important to Bambi, which was to keep his supply of Rheingold Beer ice cold in the refrigerator at all times, so that he had a can available whenever he wanted one during the day. He would stand behind the counter drinking beer and smoking all day long.

There was a payphone in the back corner against the wall, and it was my job to make sure it always had a sign on it saying "Out of Order" because Bambi wanted to be the only one to use it to talk to his wife. Normally they'd end up fighting. The fight was predictable; it was always over what he would eat when he got home.

"I don't want roast beef, Matilda. I want lasagna, Matilda."

Some customers became aware that the phone could not be out of order all the time, and they'd ask me if they could use it. When Bambi wasn't looking, I often let them. This was how I knew who was having an affair because I heard it all.

"My husband won't be home until six," etc. My lips were sealed.

About a year after I started working there, Bambi brought the most beautiful German Shepherd I had ever seen into the store. Her name was Tracy. Like most German Shepherds, Tracy was tri-colored and had beautiful markings. She had a beauty mark on the side of her face that I pointed out to Bambi once, and said, "That's because she's Elizabeth Taylor's dog." I thought Tracy looked like Rin Tin Tin. Anyway, she could have been a model or in the movies. Tracy was always on duty, and she took her job seriously. She was obedient, she listened, and she was smart. Her two ears perked up, showing that she was paying attention. Bambi loved the way I took care of Tracy. As I moved around the shop, dusting and putting cards away, he would tell Tracy to follow me around and watch me.

One day he said to me, "You know, Anthony, I want you to teach her how to walk outside without a leash on. When you go to the dumpster to throw out the garbage, I'm going to tell her to walk with you." And I thought, okay, she's pretty obedient. Tracy was right

on; she walked with me all the way around the block. I felt so proud to be with her. She had everything going for her; Bambi loved her, and I loved her. Sometimes customers would come in and be a little startled to see a German Shepherd. I would say, "No, she's fine. She won't make a move." When I'd leave the store, I'd give her a little hug on her chest, kiss her on the forehead, and say goodbye to her. Her presence added so much to the store.

One New Year's Eve, I said goodbye to Bambi, and we wished each other a great year coming up. When I came back on New Year's Day, a sign in the store said "Closed." It was dark inside. I peered through the window to see how the store could possibly be closed. It was New Year's Day, and it was going to be busy for us. Through the glass, I could see Bambi in there, and I knocked on the door. He saw me and opened the door for me to come in. He was crying hysterically. In between sobs, he told me why. The night before, someone had started drinking early at the bar across the street. Then he came over and started banging on the door of Bambi's store. Al went to the door to tell the man he was closed. When he opened the door, the man pushed his way in, and they started to fight. Tracy jumped up to protect Bambi. The man kicked Tracy in the head. She was dazed, and she wandered outside through the front door. She walked into the street where she was hit by a car. Bambi had found her dead

in the street. It was little consolation that the police arrested the drunk.

Tracy's death was traumatic for both of us. I hugged Bambi, trying to console him. He'd been up all night and was disheveled and sweaty. He went home to get some rest, and the store stayed closed for a couple of days. When it reopened, it was hard for us to get our rhythm back without Tracy there. We felt a little lost. Bambi didn't even play music anymore. About three months later, Bambi came in with a new German Shepherd.

His name was Lance, and poor Lance just didn't have what Tracy had. Lance's paws were double the size of Tracy's. His coloring wasn't right; he looked like a big black bear. One ear went up, one ear went down. He walked down the aisle with his tail wagging, knocking things off the shelves. He was not very alert, but he was lovable. Everyone who came into the store loved him. He would jump up on kids and make them laugh. I tried to train Lance, but he didn't learn. He would relieve himself in the store all the time. I cleaned up after him but didn't tell Bambi because he'd be embarrassed. Maybe it was a good thing that Lance was so different because no one could fill Tracy's paws. We did grow to love Lance and treated him kindly; we gave him a nice life. It was just a different kind of love. But we never forgot Tracy.

The Mets and the New Nun

Late in 1967, the Mets were stirring my imagination. They were planning to bring in Gil Hodges to be their new manager, and things were going to change. Gil Hodges was not only an old Dodger favorite, but he was on the original Met team at the end of his career, a beloved figure in New York—a quiet shy, no-nonsense man. I knew his presence would add discipline to the team and make the Mets play serious baseball. It was going to change everything.

Tom Seaver, twenty-two years old from Fresno, California could be the spark to set the Mets on fire. By the time the season of 1967 ended, he had won sixteen games and had an earned run average of 2.76, meaning he gave up less than three runs for every nine innings he pitched. That was phenomenal. To win that many games at twenty-two years old playing for the worst team in baseball was amazing. When the season ended, the Mets still finished dead last, winning only sixty-one games and losing 101. I was thinking that if Seaver could play that well, and with the new young players, especially the pitchers that were in the New York Met Farm System and, adding Gil Hodges as the manager,

it meant that the Mets would be taken seriously from that moment on.

Even though the Mets were loved as losers, now I had dreams of them being loved as winners. I had spent all winter waiting to see how the Mets would play in '68 when Hodges took over. In the spring of '68, they did play better. I could tell that things were starting to gel; it was no longer a sure thing that they would lose. For me, the turning point was the day I was watching a game and saw Hodges walking slowly past the pitching mound straight to the outfield where he had a discussion with the outfielder. Not even the announcers knew what was happening. We watched as the outfielder was replaced and later learned that he was taken out of the game for not hustling after the ball. That never happened again. I knew then that the Mets would not be the laughingstock of the world anymore. They were playing to win, and they had a lot more discipline. By the end of the season, the Mets finished in ninth place rather than tenth, which is last place. More impressive, they won seventy-three games. I could only dream of what would happen in April of 1969.

In September of 1968, it was announced that Gil Hodges suffered a heart attack; he was a heavy smoker. For a moment, I thought my dream was dashed, but during the off-season, he recuperated, and they said he'd be back to start the season in April 1969.

While I was working at Bambi's in the autumn of

1968, school was beginning. It was the busiest time of the year in the store. Kids needed all kinds of school supplies. I had to hustle and know what I was talking about.

I was soon to enter eighth grade. Each year before school started there was a church bazaar to raise money for the parish. This one was going to be special because it was the first year the nuns, who were in the order of the Sacred Heart of Mary, would not be wearing habits, and we would see what they looked like in civilian clothes. It was going to be startling to see the full faces of these women, their hair and their legs, all of which had been previously covered. Two other things were happening that we knew about. Sister Patrice, whom I loved and who had been my homeroom teacher for two years, was becoming the Mother Superior and would no longer be a teacher. This left an opening for a new nun, and we were curious to see her, and which students would be assigned to her.

Ed and I went to the bazaar excited to see the nuns without their habits and the new nun. When we arrived, I noticed a classmate named Carol who I had a juvenile attraction for. She said hello, and I was hoping that in the next school year we would be boyfriend and girlfriend. I wished I had an older brother who could coach me on how to act with a girl you liked. But, at that moment our goal was to find the new nun. The nuns usually walked in clusters, and we spotted the group. Sister Patrice looked just as lovely in civilian

clothes as she did in the habit. I knew I was going to miss her. I could tell by the gestures she was making that she was showing the new nun around. When I saw that nun's face, my mouth dropped and I told Ed, "Oh my God, she is the meanest, most unattractive, strictest looking person I've ever seen." The difference in looks between her and Sister Patrice was like day and night. She stood about 5'11" with broad shoulders, stiff as a board; she looked like a person who wouldn't give an inch.

I told Ed, "If I get her for homeroom teacher, my life is over. You're in the smarter class; maybe they'll give her to you. I'm in the dumb class; maybe they won't give her to me. But then again maybe they'll give her the rougher kids like me because as you can see, she could handle it." Little did I know then how the new nun would change my life.

The End of An Era

After Maria was born, my mother never visited the Mazzine house again. My father and I went alone every Sunday. I did enjoy going there except that I had to get all dressed up. The same characters would be there as my grandmother held court. I could see my Uncle Johnny Boy was going downhill and quickly. Nobody was watching his diabetes and all the other afflictions he had. It made my father sad to see his kid brother with open wounds on his hands and arms, drinking Pepsi all day and eating Drake's cakes. My father tried to talk to his mother about taking better care of him, but it was to no avail. Uncle Polack's alcoholism was taking a mighty toll, and you could tell he wouldn't be around much longer either.

In an amazing way, my father had become the black sheep of the family by living the "straight" life. I think some of his brothers thought that he was getting too uppity owning a house, working a steady job, and having a nice car with all his bills paid on time. They couldn't relate to his way of life. To them it seemed boring. When I went there, my grandmother still wanted me to go around the corner and buy her beer.

My father was against this, but she'd tell him it was okay; the man knew her, and all the kids went there to buy her beer. Out of respect for his mother, he'd let it slide. I could tell, though, that he was disgusted. Out of everyone, I knew that Grandfather Mazzine felt great pride in my father's accomplishments and the way my parents were raising me.

One Sunday when we arrived, the house was unusually quiet. As we took the walk down the long dark hallway, there was no one drinking or gambling in the dining room. It was just Johnny Boy, my grandmother, and Uncle Mikey who had a cup of coffee in his hand. I think my father and I both knew that something was up, and before we could ask, Uncle Mikey said, "That goddamn kid came here and killed the duck."

Johnny Boy mimicked Uncle Mikey, and said, "Yeah, Petie. That goddamn kid came here and killed the duck."

Hearing that, I turned to look in the living room. Grandpa Mazzine was sitting alone in his chair staring out a window; he didn't even say hello to us. My father and I were terribly upset. We were told that the "kid" was a distant relative, not a Mazzine, thank God. He was at the house, and, when my Grandfather Mazzine wasn't watching, this kid twisted the duck's neck until it broke. Grandpa Mazzine just kept staring out the window in silence. I knew the death of the duck would also be the death of Grandpa Mazzine. He had lost his best friend, along with all the attention and admiration he had received from the neighborhood. They knew him as the "Duck Man." Now that the duck was gone, it wouldn't be long before emphysema and the Chesterfields would destroy Grandpa Mazzine. The "New York's Number One Baseball Fan of 1936" was buried with the black baseball rule book he always carried in his pocket.

After his death, my father got my grandfather's Navy cap from the military. He'd always worn it when it was cold and before long, my father gave it to me. During the winter I would wear it with pride. For years, the girl, Terry, who had given me the duck would ask about it. I would tell her the duck was having a wonderful life at the Mazzine house. I had made a promise to my father not to tell her of the duck's end.

After Grandpa Mazzine died, visits to the Mazzine house were never the same. Out of respect, my father would take me to visit the rest of the family on Sundays. As I was getting a little older, I started to think about the house they all lived in. I wondered how they got along. On our visits, I'd notice that there would be several uncles still living there, but no one seemed to work. Finally on one of our rides home, I got up the courage to ask my father, "If no one works, how did they get the house?"

With a sentimental smile, he said, "I'll let you in on a little secret." He seemed proud to tell me about it, an unusual reaction for my father. The story he told gave me a deeper understanding of where I came from. He said, "Many years ago before you were born—you know the sweater factory next door to the Mazzine house? Well, the Jewish man who owns it had gotten himself in some trouble. He had been involved in an accident, and someone died. To get out of the jam he was in, he didn't need a doctor or a lawyer. What he did need was a tough Italian who would lie on the witness stand claiming to have been an eyewitness to the accident and testify that the owner of the factory was not at fault." The word on the street was that the person to see was my Grandpa Mazzine.

The man said to my grandfather, "If you lie for me on the stand and I'm acquitted, I will build a house right next door to the factory for you and all your kids." The owner of the factory was acquitted, and he built the house as he said he would with about a two-inch space between the two buildings. He had probably already owned the property. After that, whenever the man wanted to go to his summer retreat in the Catskills, Grandpa Mazzine would drive him.

Sister Elizabeth

It was clear that the freedom I'd hoped for after Maria was born was not to be. The Timex my mother had given me was to be worn at all times while I did my errands. Not only did she expect me to do all the shopping for her at the grocery stores, the butcher, the delicatessen, and the drug store, but she added something new to her list. She wanted me to buy feminine napkins for her at the drug store.

This, I said, was where I drew the line. She did not relent. She demanded that I buy these for her saying it was no big deal. We fought, but finally I gave in. I told her to write it down on a piece of paper, which she thought was ridiculous, but I thought it would save me some embarrassment. I would go around the corner and hang out in front of the drug store to make sure there was no one I knew around. When I went inside, I pretended to look at items on the shelves until I was sure I was alone. Then I would hand the man the note and on top of this, I had to tell him to please "put it in the book" because we didn't have any money. She had no idea how humiliating this was to me, or she just didn't care. My gramps wasn't around to protect me anymore, which made it worse.

My parents still wanted to have their social life so before I knew it, I started babysitting for them. At first it was a little nerve-wracking because I wanted to do everything perfectly to make sure my sister was fine. I checked her crib about every ten minutes and put my hand over her back to make sure she was still breathing. My mother taught me how to change a diaper which, thank God, I didn't have to do too much. When they went out, they called me nearly every hour to make sure everything was fine. I was okay with the babysitting because usually there was a baseball game on or, if not, I could just listen to music I liked by myself.

School started, and I believed that this was going to be the most difficult year of my life. It was my last year at St. Pius and my homeroom teacher was Sister Elizabeth! After the first day of school, Ed and I met as usual to walk home, and we discussed our first day. He got a nice man named Mr. Valar for homeroom. Sister Maureen got the average kids, and, of course, Sister Elizabeth got the "dumber" ones like me. Ed enjoyed rubbing it in. I was more depressed now than ever. I didn't think things could get much worse, from my new homeroom teacher to my mother making me her maid and my baby sister's sitter, to working at Bambi's, to my grandfather having a nervous breakdown. I felt then that I was truly alone carrying a deep sadness inside.

I had to work at Bambi's that night, but I couldn't get my mind off my new teacher. She was very strict with us the first day, said she came from Sag Harbor and was not happy about being transferred. She added that even though she wasn't happy about leaving Sag Harbor, she was going to make the most of this experience. She also said she believed there must be a reason that God had sent her to Rosedale. When I got home, my parents asked how my first day was. I said, "I got the new nun." They asked what I thought, and I said, "She's not Sister Patrice."

There was a new kid in town named Mark. He was the tallest kid in our school, and I probably was the shortest boy. He was not very bright, probably had been kept back a couple of times, and he had a hare lip. I befriended him because kids were making fun of him and calling him "Giraffe." My gramps always taught me that if someone is an underdog or being singled out, that's the person you should help. I never thought in terms of rich and poor but noticed that Mark looked like he was poor. He didn't live in a neighborhood like mine. He lived in a shack in the middle of nowhere—a place that we used to call "the swamps." It was undeveloped land. Mark said he lived with his father and his aunt. At the time I never knew anyone who was divorced, so I assumed that Mark's mother had died, and his aunt moved in to take care of him and his father. (I later learned that his "aunt" was probably his father's live-in girlfriend.) If the kids hadn't been so cruel and had given him a chance, they would have known that Mark was the kindest, most good-natured kid I ever met.

Mark seemed to have a special affection for Sister Elizabeth. He would stay after class and do small chores for her. It was hard for me to believe he wanted to spend more time with her, but since I was hanging out with him anyway, sometimes I would also stay after class for a short time. I was drawn into their company but stayed quiet and didn't say much. Sister Elizabeth treated Mark very kindly, and he probably appreciated her motherly caring. I could only be with them for ten or fifteen minutes then I would have to run, the Timex an ever-present reminder of when I had to leave and do things for my mother.

One day early on, Sister Elizabeth asked, "Where are you always running to?"

I answered that I had to work at Bambi's or go shopping for my mother.

She said, "I never see you having fun like the other kids."

I knew she was right, but I had already stayed an extra five minutes and had to run home.

When Christmas came, I was stunned when Sister Elizabeth handed me a wrapped present and said, "Open it."

I said, "Oh no, Sister, I don't have a gift for you, and

I'm really surprised by this, but I have to run and would rather open it when I'm alone."

The gift was a little Snoopy Friendship Book with "Merry Christmas" written on it. The next time I saw her, I told her I was so taken aback by her gift and that I knew how she felt about Mark, but I didn't think she even knew I existed.

She said, "I've been observing you. You are the special one." Then she said something strange. "You ought to take that off your shoulder."

I asked what she was talking about.

She said, "The world. Why are you walking around like you have the world on your shoulders?"

I answered, "Because it is."

She seemed concerned and asked if I wanted to tell her about it. I told her it was too hard to explain, but she said that she'd listen if I gave her the opportunity. Of course, in that moment, I didn't have time; I had to run.

She had said I was special. I had not heard words like that since Gramps was around. How could this be? She didn't know me; I'd been hiding behind Mark the whole time. Suddenly she didn't seem mean at all and the way I felt about her and her looks when I first saw her faded away. Was this even impossible—that a little gift and some kind words could change the way I felt about her? That Christmas break was the first time in my life I couldn't wait to go back to school. It was hard to believe, but I really missed Sister Elizabeth.

Now that I felt noticed, when Mark would stay after class, I joined in the conversations little by little. I would start opening up and saying things, and one day Sister Elizabeth asked me, "What makes you happy?"

No one had asked me that before, but I knew inside exactly what I cared about. I said, "Well I love my black mollies, music and the Mets. The three Ms." I showed her the palm of my hand on which the lines form an M, and said, "Even my hand has an M."

I told her that there was a movie I saw as a kid called *West Side Story* and I loved it. "The story's great, and the music is riveting and every day before school, I play a song from the musical on the hi fi in my basement. First, I feed my fish, then play at least one song, and then I come to school. The movie is back in the theaters after all these years."

Much to my surprise, a few days later, Sister Elizabeth said to the class, "Why don't we have a little field trip and go to the movies and see *West Side Story*, which is playing in town. Anthony Albano said it's worth seeing, and the music is beautiful." I was stunned that she mentioned my name in class. It felt so good to be acknowledged and to feel that I mattered in this world. She arranged a little trip, and several classmates went. When we walked into the movie theater, she sat down, and I took a seat leaving an empty one between her and me. As we left the theater, she said that I was right; it was a beautiful story, and the music was gorgeous.

"But I have a question for you. Why didn't you sit next to me? I don't bite."

I replied that I didn't want to look like a goody-two-shoes or a teacher's pet. The truth is I was dying to sit next to her, but I felt then everyone would see that my feelings for her were becoming strong, and I could not let anyone know how intense my emotions were.

One day when Mark and I were staying after class to talk to Sister Elizabeth, she asked me what sign I was.

I said, "I don't know."

She said, "You don't know! How could you not know what sign you are?"

"Well, I was born in April."

"I need to know the day you were born."

"The 21st."

"That makes you a Taurus, but you're on the cusp." I had no idea what "the cusp" meant.

Then she said, "I'm a Virgo, and I read my horoscope every day."

This was confusing. I said, "You're a nun. You're not supposed to believe in horoscopes. You're supposed to believe in Jesus."

"Can't you have any fun?" she said. You're such a little old man."

Somehow, I took that as a compliment.

I was starting to enjoy her company more and more and looked forward to being around her whenever I could, outside the classroom. I felt bad but I really wished Mark would disappear so that I could talk more openly to her. At first, I couldn't understand why he would want to be in her company; now I understood, and I didn't want him around. What a difference four months made. In the classroom, though, she didn't show any favoritism at all. She was all business unlike Sister Patrice who would cut me a little slack sometimes.

Before I met Sister Elizabeth, I was at my lowest point mentally and emotionally. My grandfather wasn't around, and my mother was being incredibly cruel. That she seemed to care so much about me woke up something deep inside me that I couldn't explain. One of the most important things Sister Elizabeth said to me was, "Tell me about your love of baseball. Didn't you say you loved the Mets?"

I said I did.

"Why do you like them; they lose every game. I'm from the Bronx, and I like the Yankees. They're a great team."

"Yeah," I said. "It's easy to like a winner, you and everyone else, but true love is sticking with your team, win or lose. Sister, there are nine beatitudes."

"Anthony, you know there are only eight; we taught you that in Catechism."

I said, "That's where you're wrong. The ninth beatitude is *Blessed are the Mets, for they shall inherit first place.*"

She laughed and said, "Would you like to go to some games when the season starts? We'll ask the other kids if they'd like to come."

This was almost too good to be true.

"I would love it," I said, and realized that what I was feeling for her was much more than a student is supposed to toward a teacher, but I was so happy. "That would be great. When we go to the Mets games, that will give me an opportunity to win you over to the other side."

"You're on."

Now I started to feel envious of Mark because he could stay with her as long as he wanted, and I always had to run home. I felt like I was missing out on the after-school talks. From that moment on, all I could talk about was the Mets. Every day that I stayed after school, I would give Sister Elizabeth little facts about the upcoming season. I went from saying nothing to dominating the conversation, but I only had five to ten minutes and I wanted to get it all out. During these months leading up to April, it was so important for me to let Sister Elizabeth know what the upcoming year was going to be like.

She would ask, "What makes you so sure that this year is going to different?"

I would say, "Sister, it takes years to build what the Mets have built. It's all been in the works."

One day I would tell her that Tom Seaver had

an ERA of 2.2 in 1968 and had won sixteen games. Another day, I'd tell her, that Jerry Koosman had an ERA of 2.08, and he won nineteen games. I told her about a tremendous flame thrower from Texas named Nolan Ryan who struck out 133 batters in 134 innings, and he was clocked at throwing the ball over a hundred miles an hour. After I set the stage for what was coming, I said that since they added Gil Hodges to be their manager, they had been playing to win ever since. I informed her that great pitching will always defeat great hitting. I wanted her to be a Mets fan before we ever went to the games.

She asked me, "How do you know so many statistics and so much about baseball?"

I said, "I've been studying."

She replied, "If you studied your schoolwork like this, you'd be a scholar; you'd be tops in your class!"

I was still walking home from school with Ed and several times he mentioned that I seemed to have had a change of heart about Sister Elizabeth. I said, "Ed, you know, after school she's kind of fun once you get to know her, and she even said she would take us to baseball games in April." Not wanting to show my emotions, I said, "She's still a bitch in class, though."

After school, I tried to stretch the amount of time I spent with her; it seemed to fly by so quickly. I'd look at my Timex and would be sick at heart that I had to leave. When the time stretched out to half an hour,

my mother laid down the law. She said, "Enough with after school; you have things to do. You don't have time to dilly-dally. That's why I bought you the watch."

The next day, after talking to Sister Elizabeth for five minutes, I told her, "I have to go. I can't be late getting home anymore."

She said, "Why are you always on the run?"

I said, "Sister, I feel like I've been on the run all my life."

She looked sad, and I was on my way.

I started to feel that she was becoming a believer. True to her word, we did start going to night games with a couple of other kids. At first, I was just thrilled. Each time we went, the Mets would win a nail-biter of a game. Everything seemed magical; everything was falling into place going the Mets way. For each game we went to, I'd get a scorecard and keep score of every batter, every inning, with little symbols that I'd learned from my father as a child. Sister Elizabeth asked why I needed to have the scorecard.

I told her, "Keeping the scorecard was documenting the history of the game."

Sister Elizabeth was fascinated that I was so studious. While the other kids were busy getting a hotdog or going to the bathroom, I was taking things so seriously.

She said, "You're like a little old man." Once again, I took it as a compliment.

While the Mets were playing great baseball, the nonbelievers were saying, "Let them have fun this month. Talk to me in June when they'll be in last place."

I would say, "Not this year!"

I noticed every time we went to another game, another kid would lose interest, so the number in our little group was getting smaller. I found myself wishing that all the kids would just disappear, and I thought she was thinking the same thing. Luckily, none of the kids were fanatical Mets fans like me. They might enjoy a game, whereas if I could, I would have slept at Shea Stadium. I was dreaming of the day when it would be just Sister Elizabeth and me. That day wasn't too far off. When the last kid dropped out, I was in heaven. I never told my mother that it was just Sister Elizabeth and me. She assumed other kids were going too.

The first time we went to a game alone, she said, "By the way, my name is Mary. You can call me that when we're alone." Then she took out a pack of cigarettes.

I was shocked. "You smoke?!"

She said, "If you ever tell the other kids, I'll kill you." She said she had gotten so into the Mets that she couldn't watch a game without smoking, and she'd even curse a bit if they made a mistake.

In April, on the day of my fourteenth birthday when we were alone for only a moment after school, she handed me an envelope with something heavy in it, so it was more than a card, and said, "Happy birthday."

I put it between my books and ran home to open it. When I opened it, I found an 1878 silver dollar. Not only was I shocked by the gesture of such a gift, but I knew the coin was pretty expensive for a nun who doesn't have money. I was so happy she remembered that I liked coins. I loved the silver dollar; the only problem was I couldn't show it to anyone. I was living a secret life, just as I had with Gramps when I was young.

One Small Step

Now that I really couldn't stay after school with Sister Elizabeth, and the Mets would go on road trips sometimes for as long as two weeks, it felt unbearable for us to be apart for that amount of time. The attraction and feelings we had were overflowing.

One Sunday, Mary asked me if I could help her with some school papers. I said yes before she even got the words out! I knew there was much more to this than helping her do paperwork. It was the first moment we would be together with no one else around. As I walked to meet her at the school, my heart was beating so hard that I felt it would fly out of my chest. I had one thing on my mind. This would be the day we would kiss, and I knew she felt the same way.

We were in the paper supply room with the Xerox copy machine. Still to this day, when I smell fresh cut paper and ink, I am transported back to that moment. There was a little step ladder in the small room. I got up on the ladder and said, "Look Sister, we're the same height now."

She walked toward me, and we kissed for the first time. We were very clumsy, but it was the most electrifying, clumsy kiss of my fourteen years. We would get better with more practice and practice we did. Every time we tried to say goodbye, we had to kiss each other one more time. I was so ecstatic. I don't remember doing the paperwork I went there to help her with. I couldn't believe I was kissing someone, who in September I had called the "meanest, most unattractive woman I'd ever seen."

That day she told me that she had never kissed anyone before, that she had gone straight from high school into college while being in the convent, and that she never wanted to be touched by anyone until she met me. For me, I could hardly believe that, with all the acne I had, she wanted to kiss me. I felt so ugly.

When I expressed how terrible I felt about my looks, she said, "It doesn't matter. I love who you are and what's inside of you."

That helped me tremendously to be less embarrassed, but I still didn't believe her.

After that, when I had to sit through class during the day, it was more difficult than ever to concentrate on school. All I could think about was being in love with Sister Elizabeth, and, of course, the Mets. Mary and I would have to get creative about seeing one another and, of course, with the utmost secrecy. I was afraid that my friends, Mark or Ed, would find out. I knew Mark still spent time with Sister Elizabeth every day after school alone, and I was happy he had that time to himself with her. Ed and I still walked home from school together, but since we both were working at Bambi's we didn't have much time to hang out. Luckily, neither one of them cared to go to a baseball game.

I did notice that Ed had become quite popular with the boys in school all of a sudden. I could not figure this one out. How did he become the man of the boys of the eighth grade? Then it became abundantly clear. One night when I was working at Bambi's I went to throw out the trash in the dumpster behind the store. In it I saw brand new items laying in the garbage and a whole stack of the latest edition of Playboy Magazine. Ed was storing these items to sell them at school. The next day I told him I knew how he had become the overnight sensation. I also told him I couldn't believe he would steal from Bambi who treated us so well. In my most serious voice, I said that I wouldn't rat him out this time, but if I ever saw this going on again, I was going to tell Bambi. After that, our friendship was fractured, and we did not spend time together anymore.

Now I could see Sister Elizabeth without wondering if Mark or Ed suspected anything. Even though the Mets were playing better, they still were just playing 500 baseball. I always had to remind her that it was a long season, and we were only in May. It was a long time until late September, and it was better to start off like this and get momentum later on. The main thing was it was no longer taken for granted that they would lose.

With one month left to be part of the first graduating class of St. Pius the 10th, Mary and I would have to be very careful about when we saw each other and steal away any moment we could find. Then out of nowhere, my mother said that she had premier tickets to the movie, "Funny Girl," opening at Radio City Music Hall, and she didn't feel well and wouldn't be going. She said, "Why don't you take your teacher, the nun? You know the one who took you to all the baseball games?"

Not wanting to give myself away, I said, "I don't know how I feel about that—going alone with my teacher to Manhattan."

My mother said, "I'll even give you extra money so you can go out to dinner with her. Nuns don't have any money, and this would show your appreciation for the games she took you to. It'll be a real treat for her."

By this time, I knew the phone number of the convent. So, I called and in a very low-key way, with my mother standing there, I said, "Would you like to go to a movie in Manhattan? My mother wants to treat you."

On her end, she had to be low-key as she checked with the other nuns to see if there was a car available that night. This was a heaven-sent gift to both of us. She asked me to put my mother on the phone. "I want to thank her for this."

Mary picked me up in the Pontiac Lemans that belonged to the convent, and we went to the "Funny

Girl" premier and out to dinner together. The good feelings between my mother and Sister Elizabeth were not destined to last long because only days later, we all had to attend my cousin's confirmation. The day after the ceremony, Sister Elizabeth said to me, "Do you think your mother could stop chewing gum long enough to get through the service?"

I was totally mortified and embarrassed for my mother. I was so hurt to think that Mary viewed my mother in a bad light, and that she would bring it to my attention. When I got home, infuriated over the whole incident, I scolded my mother and said, "Did you have to chew gum while you were in church?"

She said, "What do you care?"

I said, "Well, Sister Elizabeth said you were chewing gum during the whole ceremony."

Her reply was, "Tell the goddam nun to mind her own friggin' business!"

I Still Don't Understand

With weeks to go before graduation, my mother laid down the law about my grades telling me that if she found any red marks on my report card, there would be hell to pay. In St. Pius the 10th, passing was a 70 in any given subject. If it went below 70, it was written in red. I knew she made this statement because of the time I was spending with Sister Elizabeth. At first, my parents thought that I would do better in school now that a teacher was showing interest in me and my grades would reflect that. It seemed every time I left the house, my mother would say, "There better not be any red marks."

While Sister Elizabeth and I were laying low, the Mets were flying high. Before I knew it, the Mets won three straight, six straight, nine straight, then eleven straight games. Of course, that winning streak was a record for the Mets. Bambi was good enough to let me listen to the games while I was working, and some of his customers were starting to make comments while they were shopping. Some would wait until the inning was over before they left to go home to catch the rest of the game. Sometimes someone would thank Bambi for having the game on.

Being a good businessman, he would say, "Of course, I would have it no other way. They are our Mets!" When that customer left, he would get a role of paper towels and throw it at me and say, "I did it for you, Anthony."

The Mets were even starting to stir the imaginations of people who never really cared about baseball before. The non-believers would try to discourage me telling me to wait until July to see where the Mets would be. And I would reply, "Not this year."

While the Cubs were sitting in first place, the fiery controversial manager, Leo Durocher, was asked what he thought of the Mets doing so well. He would say, in the infamous words that would haunt him for the rest of the season, "Nice guys finish last."

Now the only time I was seeing Sister Elizabeth outside of school was when I would get off from work. She would be waiting for me in the Pontiac Lemans around the corner just so that we could have that moment to be alone. We would talk about the Mets and sometimes take a ride to one of our favorite places, Carvel Ice Cream. Of course, we would make out in the car. When you're in love for the first time, it's so difficult to say goodbye if you only have an hour.

Soon, report card day came along. Sister Elizabeth had said that if anyone wanted to talk about their grade, they could stay after school and talk to her. Just

about everyone left, seemingly happy. There were two kids that spoke to her for a couple of minutes and then it was just me and her. There was one failing grade on my report; it was 69 in English, which was the subject Sister Elizabeth taught. It was better than the 65 I usually received, but I couldn't believe she would fail me for one point. I knew it wouldn't stop me from graduating, but I felt angry and emotional.

I said, "Do you know what kind of havoc this is going to cause in my house or for me?"

She said, "I crunched the numbers all different ways, and I just couldn't give you more than a 69."

"You couldn't give me one point to save me all this trouble?"

She said, "It wouldn't be fair to the other students."

Still stunned, I said, "One point? You couldn't find it in your heart?"

She said, "You should have tried harder."

"Well, I have work, and I'm spending the rest of the time making out with you. I should get a point just for that!"

Our words were bouncing back and forth like ping pong balls. I know I was red at that point. I said, "You're such a goody-two-shoes."

She tried to be kind and apologized, saying, "I'm sorry you're disappointed, but I cannot show favoritism to you over the other students. Someday you'll understand that it's all about fairness."

I believe that there are gray areas in life, and sometimes bending the rules a little to save a lot of pain is okay. I looked back at this incident when I was twenty years old and when I was thirty, and even now as I look back fifty years later, I still don't understand.

Graduation day came and went. I was still stung by the one point that gave me a failing grade. My mother's punishment was that I could not go out for the rest of the summer. I still had to run my errands for her and work at Bambi's so I was quiet and went along, but I knew this wouldn't last. I think she almost felt bad for me that I failed by one point. By the time July rolled around, life was back to normal at home. I still wanted to see Sister Elizabeth whenever I could. And, of course, go to baseball games. The two had become the most important things in my life.

Getting time off from work without my parents knowing was easy because since I had caught Ed stealing, he was very cooperative when I asked him either to work for me or switch shifts. Now that I wasn't in school anymore, it became easier for me to call Sister Elizabeth, Mary. I didn't have to be on my guard afraid of slipping in front of a student. I called Mary at the convent to see when we could go to our next game explaining that now was more important than ever. The Mets were starting to gel just in time. In early July, the Mets were about to play their first crucial game in their history. The next six games would

be against Leo Durocher's Chicago Cubs who were in first place. The Cubs had a lot of stars on their team—Ernie Banks, Billy Williams, and a great pitching staff. The Mets really didn't have a star other than Tom Seaver who was still quite young and could only pitch every fourth game.

The Mets won two of the three at home. In game two, Tom Seaver was pitching a perfect game. I was watching at home alone in my room. From the fifth inning on, I was pacing with every pitch that he threw. When the ninth inning came, I was a bunch of nerves. He was about to perform one of the rarest feats in baseball—a perfect game, which means the pitcher retires 27 straight batters meaning no one ever reaches first base. He retired the first batter. He had two more batters to get out and then a last-minute substitute named Jimmy Qualls hit a soft single to center field. It was heartbreaking; Seaver had come so close. I cried. I was not alone. There were many people crying in the stands. At that moment, everyone in the stadium stood and showed their appreciation for his accomplishment by giving him the longest standing ovation I ever heard. It took Seaver a while to regain his composure; he was quite emotional

It was unbelievable. We had come so far from being losers. He retired the next two men and had pitched a masterpiece. The next week the Mets went to Chicago and again beat them two out of three. When the

dust settled, who could believe that the Mets were in striking distance of first place, three and a half games behind the Cubs?

Now when Mary and I went to a game, I was not happy sitting up in the bleachers. We used to pay a little over a dollar to get in for general admission. With the Mets playing so much better, not only were the regular fans coming, but others intrigued by how the Mets were playing were filling up the stadium. The next time we went to get tickets before the game, I went up to the booth and asked the man in the ticket booth for the best seats he had. I wanted to be close to the action. He said there were no good seats left. Then I remembered something my father taught me years earlier. With Mary standing next to me, I said, "Johnny, I'm taking my teacher to the game. Make me look good, and here's a couple of bucks for you."

My father called everyone he didn't know "Johnny" because no matter what their name really was, he believed it was a sign of friendly familiarity with the person, almost as if you already knew him. It worked. Magically there were now good seats available. We went in and showed our ticket stubs and a man brought us to our seats, practically on ground level, brushed them off, and I gave him fifty cents.

Mary said, "I can't believe we got these seats. How did you do this?"

I told her that I gave the man a couple of extra dollars.

She said, "Well, that's not fair. You have to pay extra to get good seats?"

I turned to her and said with a serious expression, "That's how the world operates. You've been sheltered all your life."

I explained that I wanted good seats and was willing to pay a little extra for them.

She said, "I still don't think that's fair."

I said, "Someday maybe you will understand."

It's Getting Better

All the years I loved the Mets, a common sentiment among a lot of people was, "They will put a man on the moon before the Mets win a championship."

They were right. On July 20, 1969, a man landed on the moon. My own block, neighborhood, and country were preparing for this historic occasion. In our backyard, neighbors began to gather starting in the late afternoon, and they stayed well into the evening before the televised event. The whole conversation revolved around the moon landing. While everyone was talking, I heard my mother ask if you could see them land just by looking up at the moon.

Personally, I was over the moon—in love! The landing didn't interest me. My attention was consumed thinking about my Mets and their progress, and the day Mary and I could go to the next game. I was intrigued by how Gil Hodges maneuvered the team; he had some moves that were nothing short of genius. I thought I knew baseball, but he did things I'd never seen done before. For instance, when a real power hitter came up to bat, one who always pulled the ball to one side, he had all his players move over to that side of the field leaving half of the field empty. It was a gamble, but it seemed to work every time. The batter inevitably hit the ball right in the direction that Hodges had placed his players. He also installed the platoon system, meaning when a right-handed pitcher was starting, he would load the line-up with left-handed batters, and vice versa. Players that were not household names would come through with a clutch hit making them the stars of the day. Of course, the young pitching was phenomenal. The Mets still didn't score many runs, but they didn't have to because they didn't allow many runs. So many games were won by one or two runs. Most games were filled with suspense and had people holding onto their seats. There weren't many blowouts.

I didn't have high school on my mind, even though it was only a month and a half away. Ed and I would be going to different high schools. That had been decided before we graduated when we took a test to see if we were eligible to go to a Catholic school, which really meant if you were smart enough. When I took the test, I didn't really try; I was afraid my parents could not afford it anyway. Somehow, I almost made the cut. But almost making the cut did not get me in. I would be going to a public high school where racial tension filled the halls. But that was okay with me. My friendship with Ed was on the rocks anyway, and it seemed that summer Ed had found himself a new set of friends.

For me, it was just Mary and the Mets. Now that I was in love, certain popular songs would come out that turned into "our" songs. The first that became our song was "It's Getting Better" by Mama Cass Elliot. The words were so fitting.

I once thought that when love came to me
It would come with rockets, bells and poetry
But with me and you
It just started quietly and grew

On some hot summer days, Mary would drive us to the beach, and we would stroll along the boardwalk. We must have looked like an odd couple—me, a short, skinny, fourteen-year-old in a T-shirt and shorts beside a twenty-seven-year-old, tall woman with broad shoulders in conservative attire, her auburn hair shaped in an out-of-date style. We were envious of people who could show their affection openly even by just holding hands. I dreamed that one day we could also.

I was still wearing the Timex, which drove me crazy. I didn't want to be on my mother's time, doing the shopping and her errands. But now it was easier to spend more time with Mary because school was out, and I had my arrangement with Ed. When I did babysit for my sister, it gave me an opportunity to talk to Mary over the phone. When you're in love, there's so much to talk about.

One night we made plans to go out the next day for a ride, and on that hot sunny summer day, while we were driving to the beach "Sweet Caroline" played on the radio. We sang along even putting the *dum-dum-*

dums in place for effect. I had my arm out the window and the wind was gently pushing against my palm. At that moment, I thought life could never get better than this—to be free and singing along with someone you love was a feeling like no other. Never short for words, our conversations touched on every topic, and it always flowed. Mary posed a question. She wanted to know how I felt about people living together before they got married. It was the beginning of an era when people were experimenting with approaches to being together other than marriage. Some people were asking, "Why do we need a piece of paper to show our love for each other?"

I told Mary that I thought it was a terrible idea. I didn't like people shacking up with one another.

She turned to me and said, "I think you're older than me. How did I end up with a little old man?"

During the end of July and early August, the Mets started slipping a bit. It was their first real slump of the season. Mary was concerned and wondered if the dream was over. I assured her that a team usually has a slump sometime during the year. It's all about momentum; I told her that it was better it was happening now during the summer than in September.

Of course, while the Mets started to fall behind, the nonbelievers were saying, "I told you it wouldn't last."

I would quietly say, "This year is different." My heart told me that all of this excitement and enthusiasm couldn't be for nothing. And I was in love, a state where possibilities have no limits.

One night when I got off work from Bambi's, I met Mary just to spend a half hour with her kissing. Something that night made our kisses feel electric; I felt a current surging through my whole body that was different from any other time. When I was ready to kiss her one more time and pull myself out of the car, my hair was standing up on my arms, and I felt like my body was floating. I could see in her eyes the sadness that this moment had to end and that I was always on the run.

Living a secret life can be exciting but scary at times. On one of our regular evening visits to Carvel Ice Cream, after we had finished our cones, we stayed in the parking lot and began to kiss. Without any thought, for the first time I just did what came naturally, which was to put my hands on her breasts over her blouse. Of course, I was thrilled until, as I was leaning over her, I glanced out the rear-view window and saw a police car pointing in our direction parked underneath a tree. I said, "Mary, while we we're doing this, I think the cop has been watching us the whole time."

We both were frightened. I sat back in my seat telling her to just keep calm and drive away slowly. Sure enough, he followed us onto Sunrise Highway. She drove a little further, and he turned on his lights to pull us over. We were both wrecks. What would this mean? I thought we were finished. Catastrophic thoughts filled my mind—the nuns at the convent, my parents, visions of being at the police station. At the car window, the cop asked Mary for her license. It identified her as Sister Elizabeth. He looked at it carefully, then pointed the flashlight at me and asked who I was.

Mary said, "He's one of my students."

The expression on his face was one of bewilderment. I sat in silence wondering what would happen next. It was probably only a few seconds, but it felt like forever. Finally, he shook his head and said, "Lady, I'll tell you what I'm going to do. I'm going to make believe I never saw this. And please, just drive away!"

Cherish

Although that night with the police officer had us shaking in our boots, it seemed nothing could keep us apart. I was becoming a little paranoid about what people might know or what they were thinking. One day I bumped into Ed and his new set of friends. I was embarrassed when they asked me if I wanted to join them in getting into some mischief.

Ed told them, "Don't waste your time. He's only interested in hanging out with a nun."

I didn't care about his young hoodlum pals, but I wondered what Ed knew or surmised. Mary had told me that some nuns at the convent were voicing displeasure over our relationship. One nun, in particular, was concerned that it was inappropriate that we were spending so much time alone together. They also were not happy that we were dominating the use of one of the two cars at their disposal. We had thought perhaps by not trying to hide the fact that we were spending time together, it would look to others like an innocent relationship, and people's minds wouldn't go to dark, taboo places.

One afternoon, Mary asked if I'd like to take a ride to visit her parents, who lived about an hour north of us. She assured me that we could watch the game there since we were already listening to it on the radio. She said it would mean a lot to her. I agreed, and she called ahead to let them know we were coming. She seemed excited. I went along just to be in her company. We arrived at a large apartment building in Bronxville. The apartment itself was small and the furniture and décor looked like it hadn't changed since the 1950s. I noticed something odd in Mary's girlish smile and her shyly proud expression when she introduced me to her parents. It was as if she was bringing her first boyfriend home for them to meet.

Her mother was sweet, gracious, and refined. She said she'd heard a lot about me. But her father, a bus driver, just sat in his armchair not saying much; he seemed puzzled by the appearance of this boy in his house. Mary tried to get us to make small talk; the game was on television, and she pressed me to explain some baseball facts and tidbits to her father, but he wasn't interested. I was polite, but I couldn't break the ice with him. Both her parents had Irish accents, but her father's was much stronger, and with the little he did say, I found it difficult to understand him. Mary's mother offered me a yogurt, which I had never had before. It tasted terrible. Only later did I learn that I should have stirred it to get the full flavor.

As we walked away from their apartment, Mary

pointed out the spot where she had been bitten by a dog when she was young. That explained why she was so terrified of dogs. Whenever we passed one, she would hide behind me and scream if the dog got too close to her. She couldn't believe that I could easily make friends with a dog I didn't know. It would make her sick if I let the dog lick me on the face. I would try to make her more comfortable by holding a dog and offering for her to pet its back. She would try, but she was so uncomfortable I didn't want to push it.

As the Mets were still in their slump, falling nine and a half games behind the Cubs, I didn't give up hope, fully believing there had to be a reason we had gotten this far. It helped that Mary wanted to get away for a weekend and visit her old convent and school out in Sag Harbor on Long Island. Of course, since we were going for a weekend, we had to bring a couple of other kids. Two of them had accompanied us to baseball games. Mark also came. It was great to be with him again, and I let his wonderful, outgoing personality lead the way.

When we drove on to the grounds, as I looked around at the perfectly placed ancient trees, I realized what a special place it was. The convent itself was the most beautiful structure I had ever been in. One nun came down the ornate wooden staircase to greet us. I could see why Mary never wanted to leave this place that used to be her home. All the sisters were happy to see her and she to see them. A big picture window in the living room looked out over the water and a narrow pier that jutted straight out from the shore. I could see Mary and the kids at the end of the pier. Mary was wearing a bathing suit. Everybody was having the time of their lives. As for me, I enjoyed being inside looking out the window, rocking in my chair, and taking it all in. I had never known the peace that I felt in that moment. Later, I found what I thought was a perfect shell. On the ride home, the song, "Cherish," came on the radio. I asked everyone to be quiet as I listened. I wanted to sing the lyrics out loud. "Cherish is the word I use to describe you . . ." I knew Mary understood that these words were for her. When I got home, I wrote 1969 on the shell in black magic marker. It's been fifty years now, but it still sits on my bookshelf.

Soon after we came home from Sag Harbor, many people just a little older than me were headed north to the Woodstock Music Festival in the little town of Bethel, New York. It was to be a weekend of peace-loving music. Unfortunately, as I was only fourteen at the time, I didn't understand the gravity of this spontaneous gathering of humanity, but it certainly had more of an interest and fascination for me than the moon landing, perhaps because it was more of a New York happening. The newspaper headlines and television coverage were endless, calling the concert location a disaster area. The customers coming into Bambi's were split; some people thought it was a disgrace creating nothing but havoc, and others thought it was wonderful to see a generation taking care of themselves and having a good time. Probably those were the ones whose children were there. All Bambi kept saying was, "They're all hippy-snippies, naked, and on dope."

I started thinking of that weekend of August 15th, 16th, and 17th and how marvelous it was that no one was fighting, and people were all getting along with real community spirit. Even some people who lived in the upstate neighborhoods were kind to the concertgoers. They were inconvenienced by all the people flooding into their area, but they were tolerant. On the first night, a fairly unknown twenty-two-year-old singer-songwriter named Melanie performed. I didn't know it then, but she would soon play a major role in my life. Even though it's fifty years later and I was not physically there, I like to think that in my day-to-day life, there is a piece of Woodstock that lives within me ethically and spiritually.

Although the New York State Thruway was closed, the good vibes must have floated down south 100 miles to the City, for that weekend the Mets broke out of their slump and then won nine out of the next ten games. By the end of August, they had climbed back into contention and the Cubs were once again in striking distance. If the game was on and I had to go to the store for my mother, I had the transistor radio glued to my ear. I didn't want to miss even one pitch of this crucial time. Sometimes in the stores, the radio reception was poor, and I'd find myself twisting, turning and contorting my body to be in just the right position to hear the game. Sometimes, too, the receptions I received from the pharmacist or butcher were also poor as they would remind me that the amount of money my mother owed them was getting out of hand. Of course, this embarrassed me greatly.

Mary was becoming more frustrated with the demands my mother imposed on me and was especially upset when she learned that I had to go to the bank for money orders because my parents never had a checking account. Strangely enough, when Mary said negative things about my mother, I wanted to defend her—she was still my mother, after all. In contrast, Mary would always remind me that she thought my father was a good man. I didn't see that clearly because my mother always tried to put a wedge between him and me by warning me not to grow up to be like him or his family. It's sad, but it took me into adulthood to realize what a good man and great father he was.

With only a couple of days left in August, I walked to the convent to bring Mary a birthday present. I had been feeling isolated in my secret life. The excitement I used to feel had turned into anxiety about being discovered. I was a little shaky as I headed toward the convent but had been listening to a new song, "Everybody's Talking at Me," by Fred Neal sung by Nilsson, which was speaking the words that fit my situation, and it made me feel protected from the isolation.

I rang the doorbell and, of course, the nun who

was most annoyed by our relationship opened the door. Mary came down to greet me and for the first time, she led me through the living quarters. I tried to take it all in without meeting anyone's eyes, but it went by quickly and, before I knew it, I was in a little office in the corner. I still had the feeling that my presence was an intrusion and not appreciated. This was the first and only time I saw where they lived. All the other times I was sent straight to the basement and Mary would join me there. I think, because it was her birthday, she felt it was okay to bring me upstairs into the living quarters, and once inside, I got the feeling we were two teenagers in love with her parents just outside the door.

When we were alone in the office, I handed Mary her present. I had chosen three 45 rpm singles. The songs were symbolic of my love for her. They were "Sweet Caroline," "Galveston," and, of course, "Cherish." Still feeling a little uncomfortable, wondering what the other nuns were thinking, I broke the ice with some humor. I told Mary I wasn't going to give her cigarettes for her birthday, and I certainly was not going to get a card with Virgo, her horoscope sign, on it. She laughed. She played the song, Cherish, and when she did, I told her, "Every time you play that song, remember those are the words I feel about you." She blushed and the look on her face told me that no one had ever said anything like that to her before.

She said softly, "Yes, that will always be our song."

When I left the office and convent, I was grateful

I still had the song, "Everybody's talking at me, I don't hear a word they're saying. . ." to protect me for the walk home.

So far it had been an amazing summer—the moon landing, Woodstock, and people praying for peace while young men were being sent to war. My lovable losing Mets were doing great, and I was in love. My mother's cruelty was becoming less effective and could not penetrate the feeling and spirit inside me. And, while necking in the Pontiac Lemans, Mary and I made the summer heat hotter than it already was.

I was ready for September, and it would be like no other.

Nothing's Gonna Stop Us Now

With one week away from school opening, my mind should have been on what going to a public high school for the first time would be like. But it also was the biggest time of the year for Bambi's Stationery Store, and my mind was consumed by helping shopping mothers get their children ready for school and the Mets. If a game was on, I tried my best to concentrate on the customer while at the same time having one ear on the game.

Since Labor Day landed on September 1st that year, school was starting late. That week, for the first time, my father seemed quite concerned that I was going to an integrated high school where there was a lot of racial tension and fighting. I wasn't a fighter, and he was worried for my safety. He rarely expressed his apprehension, but this time told me he wished I'd done better on the test making me eligible for a Catholic high school. He would have felt better if I were going to Holy Cross like my friend Ed. He said that if I had been accepted, he would have gotten the money from Uncle Frank to make it possible. But I felt confident that I had learned to navigate the world by watching the Mazzines, and I would be fine.

The first week of September, all I dreamed and wished for was for the Mets to just hang in there until September 8th when the Chicago Cubs were coming to New York to play two games. My prayers were answered. They more than hung in there. When that Monday morning arrived, they were only two and a half games behind. While the Cubs were falling flat, the Mets were on a tear—they had momentum.

That morning for my first day at Springfield Gardens High, I waited for the bus; it was my first time taking public transportation to school. I met some of the kids from St. Pius the 10th that used to hang out with Ed and me, but I hadn't seen them since Mary had come into my life. On the ride to school, I was wishing that I would be able to go to the most-important-ever game that night. While I should have been getting oriented at my new school, as the day dragged on, I could only think of how I would get to that game. I was bubbling with enthusiasm like I never had before. I had become obsessed. Finally, when the last bell rang, all I wanted to do was to call Mary as soon as I got home. With no time to waste, I moved quickly to catch the first bus. When I arrived home, my parents asked how the first day had gone. As I rushed to my room, I said that it went fine. I put my books down and changed my clothes. My next move was to call Mary. Within minutes, I was out of the house and running to the pay phone on the corner. As I dialed the convent phone number—by now I knew it by heart—I was hoping Mary would answer the phone, but she didn't. Of course, the person who answered was the nun most annoyed with our relationship. When Mary got to the phone, I explained how important it was for us to go to the game.

She said, "You caught me off guard. Why didn't you let me know sooner?" She hadn't put in to have the car and it also looked like rain. "You know, some of the other nuns are getting very upset."

I said, "I know that, but it's very important that we go tonight because the whole season hinges on tonight's game."

She said, "Okay, call me back in fifteen minutes. I'll see what I can do." She mentioned the rain again.

I said, "Don't worry about the weather. God would never let it rain tonight."

I ran back to the house to wait the fifteen minutes before running back to the pay phone. When I called, she told me that she had gotten the car for the night, and we were set. I thanked her and asked if she could pick me up early at about six o'clock explaining that I expected a big crowd would be there, and I wanted us to have good seats. I went back home and paced back and forth in my bedroom. I was a bundle of nerves. It was as if my life depended on getting to that game. Maybe it did. I told my parents that my teacher was willing to take me to the game that night. And, for the first time that season, my father said, "Your Mets are doing great."

He handed me some extra money without my mother noticing and reminded me to slip the ticket man a couple of extra bucks to get us good seats. I told him I had not forgotten. He seemed excited for me and, just as the car pulled up, he said, "Make sure that you pay for your teacher. Never let a woman pay for you." As I walked toward Mary's car, my father said, "Anthony, I hope they win!"

September 8th turned out to be my personal Woodstock. Even though it had only been two days since I last saw Mary, it seemed like a long time. I got into the car and thanked her for making this night possible on such short notice, emphasizing the urgency I felt growing as the school day dragged on. Of course, when you're in love, even time takes on a new meaning. The forty-five-minute ride to Shea Stadium seemed to go by in ten. Song after song playing on the radio symbolized our relationship. The first song was "Those Were the Days, My Friend," and the last was "Turn, Turn, Turn." When it came to the last sentence, I sang a little louder and directly at Mary "... a time for peace, I swear it's not too late." She was surprisingly impressed when I told her the words were from the Bible, the Book of Ecclesiastes. I told her that Pete Seeger had put the words to the melody.

She said, "You're so smart. You just don't apply yourself in school."

Driving into the parking lot, we could see, through the huge opening of the ballpark, the floodlights and the stands in the stadium. Over the years I had seen that same spot many times, but this time was different. My anticipation and excitement were magnified. I had goosebumps and showed Mary the hair standing up on my arms. Who could believe my lovable losers only a short time ago were considered the worst team in baseball? Now they were about to play two games with the Cubs for first place. All the naysayers predicted they couldn't last until May, and with each passing month they moved the goal post. Now with less than a month left, they not only shocked the baseball world, but the whole sports world. The sun finally came out, and it was good that we arrived early because others had too, and there were many more people than usual. Mary was surprised because it was a Monday evening and the first day of school. I had already forgotten that I'd attended my first day in high school. I did as my father suggested and threw the ticket attendant more money than usual. We got great seats with plenty of time left before the game started. Everyone in the stands was extra-chatty; we became friendly neighbors as if we'd known one another all our lives.

At eight o'clock, Jane Jarvis played the organ like she had done before every Mets game to the Mets theme song, "Meet the Mets." With the words flashing on the scoreboard, the crowd sang like never before. The table was set, and the Mets were going to start their young pitcher, Jerry Koosman from Minnesota, who had learned how to pitch the ball by throwing it against his barn wall. He had been phenomenal all year and retired the Cubs easily in the top of the first inning. Tommy Agee, the lead-off hitter, came to bat. Then a strange thing happened. The first pitch thrown by the Cubs pitcher was aimed at Agee's head. He had to twist and turn to get out of the way of the fast ball. His head went one way and the bat another as he fell on the ground to avoid getting hit by the ball. It was Leo "the Lip" Durocher doing what he did best intimidating the batter and the Mets. He had ordered a purpose pitch to aim for the batter's head. He would regret that move, for two innings later, Tommy Agee hit a ball over the center field fence 410 feet away, and justice was served as the Mets were then winning 2-0. It was great to a have two-run lead, but it was a shaky lead because the Cubs had a lot of heavy hitters. The game was tense. Each inning and each pitch were so important. Koosman, showing Durocher he was not intimidated, threw the pitch at one of their stars, Ron Santo, and hit him.

Mary was totally caught up in the fever of the game. When she wasn't smoking, she was holding onto my arm or leg with every pitch. Koosman seemed to be coasting like he had done all season, but the Cubs put together a couple of hits and tied up the game. It was now 2-2, the bottom of the sixth. I was happy I had taught Mary so much about baseball during the season because she didn't ask any questions that would take my focus off the game.

With Tommy Agee up again, he hit a ball to left field and, while watching the outfielder take his time, Agee rounded first and turned it into a double. The outfielder's slowness was exactly the kind of play Hodges used to hate when he took over the Mets, and they played that way. Now the Mets played aggressively and hustled, and, in this case, the Cubs lack of hustling worked for the Mets. With the go-ahead run on second, the large crowd was on the edge of their seats. The next batter hit a single and Agee, who never thought about stopping, rounded third. It was a gamble, but he was coming home. Everyone knew the ball and Agee would be arriving at home plate at the same moment. With Agee running full tilt, some people held their breath, some closed their eyes. Mary was screaming, "Anthony, God Almighty, let him be safe."

I stood and gave the safe signal as if my will could make the call happen, and when the umpire called, "Safe," I believed I had done it. While the crowd let go a big sigh of relief and was gleefully jumping up and down in the stands, Durocher stormed out of the dugout screaming with the Cub players joining him to try to convince the umpire that Agee was out. The longer they argued, the more the Mets fans booed. Gil Hodges, the quiet stern man, just sat calmly in the dugout. If you were a Cubs fan, I'm sure you would think Agee was out at home, but we were Mets fans, and these were the kind of calls that always went against us in the earlier years. It was poetic justice that the player, Tommy Agee, who they had tried to intimidate by throwing the ball at his head with the first pitch was the player who singlehandedly beat them. But this year there was magic in the air and, during the seventh inning stretch, fans sang "Take Me Out to the Ballgame" like I'd never heard it sung before. Two more innings and the Mets would be getting closer to the impossible dream. Once again, the young pitching staff held on, and the Mets won the game by one run like they had done all year, 3-2.

I had just witnessed the greatest game I ever attended! When it was over, the fans did not want to leave the stands; they didn't want to stop soaking in this tremendous feeling. It was the first time I didn't see people running to their cars after a game to drive away to beat the traffic. Over the loudspeaker the announcer's voice was saying, "The game is over. Please drive home safely." When we finally left the stands, the celebration continued. You could feel the buzz as we walked down the cement ramps to exit the stadium. I was so happy that I showed my affection for Mary openly, holding her hand and putting my arm around her tall body. I didn't even care about my acne. She was sharing this joyful moment. We were all on cloud nine. In the parking lot, the lights were still on and we could still hear the announcer saying, "The game is over. Please drive home safely."

But no one drove away. Everyone was hanging out talking about the game and congratulating one another as the celebration continued. Then one person put the key in his ignition and from his radio blasted the song, "Everybody Get Together, Try to Love One Another Right Now." Then everyone, Mary included, did the same thing and the song streamed out of every parked car with the whole crowd singing along and flashing peace signs at each another. Some people were smoking pot. At that moment, we were all in it together. It was my Woodstock. It had that outpouring of warm feeling that made you believe the war would end. I was grateful to be one of the 44,000 people at that game. If you were at that game, I'm sure you've never forgotten it. I was confident that nothing was going to stop us now. When we finally drove away, I told Mary, "We have it now."

She said, "Momentum?"

I responded, "No, now it's destiny."

Flying High

That night I didn't want to break the spell by falling asleep. The game with all its magic replayed in my mind over and over again. Living on pure adrenalin, it was no problem to get up and ready for my second day of school. Once again, the school day dragged, and on the bus home, even the ride seemed longer. Before I got home, I stopped off at the pay phone dialing the convent's number to thank Mary for taking me to the greatest game of my life. She also was still flying high. It was Tuesday night, and my father didn't have to go to his second job. So, when I walked through the door, he said, "That was some game last night. Did the nun enjoy it?"

I said she did and told him that she was even screaming at times, and it was a little embarrassing. It wasn't true at all that I was embarrassed, but because of my paranoia about my parents or others learning the true nature or our relationship, I threw that in to make it seem like Mary and I were in a purely innocent friendship.

Feeling confident about the future of the Mets, I was content to watch the game Tuesday night from home. Surprisingly, my father was interested also; he had been quiet all season, but it seemed like now he was caught up in the excitement. That night did not have the drama of the night before. But as always with the Mets, expect the unexpected. The game was held up because a black cat would not get off the field. The groundskeepers kept trying to catch him but ended up falling on top of each other. And before the cat was ready to leave, he went up to Leo Durocher and hissed at him live on television. Then he ran under the stands and the crowd was thrilled. It was the first time I saw people not get upset when a game was delayed.

With Tom Seaver on the mound, the Mets made it look easy beating the Cubs 7-1. Before the game was over, 55,000 people in the stadium sang, "Goodnight Leo, we hate to see you go," to the tune of "Good Night Ladies" all waving white handkerchiefs. The Cubs were so upset that they claimed the Mets put the black cat on the field on purpose to jinx them. After the Mets finished them off, the Cubs limped back to Chicago looking like a beaten team. Mrs. Joan Whitney Payson, the matriarch and owner of the Mets and the woman who made this all possible, sat in her regular box seat by the Mets' dugout wearing one of her wonderful hats. The next day in the newspaper, it was reported that Mrs. Payson decided to surprise the players by coming into the locker room with her entourage. The players who were naked all had to cover up. It was the first time a woman had ever come into a locker room, and she was their boss. She said hello to all the players, but her real purpose was to see Gil Hodges in his office. She was crying as Gil Hodges, being the gentleman he was, stood up and took off his hat. She kissed him on the forehead thanking him and telling him, "You have made me so very happy." She also said, "I'll see you tomorrow night when we are in first place."

Mrs. Joan Whitney Payson was right. On Wednesday night, September 10th the Mets won a double-header against Montreal, and the Cubs kept losing. For the first time in their history, the Mets were fully in first place alone. Once again, I was content to watch the game at home on television. Seeing the rip-roaring crowd filled to capacity brought me great joy. In the late innings, the scoreboard flashed, "Look Who's in First Place." And every one of the 55,000 people began to shout, "We're number one!" I got choked up seeing that and went into my room to be alone. I had a good cry and felt wonderful to finally let out all that pent-up emotion. Not only for this season, but all the years following and loving my Mets. I dreamt a dream that was so unrealistic and so far out of reach, and it came true. I think I was the only one more emotional than Mrs. Payson. Plus, I was in love.

After the game, I listened to the post-game report, like always. Then to cap off a wonderful evening, it was time to calm down and listen to some music. I turned on the radio, and, of course, the first song that played was "Cherish."

Thursday and Friday nights, I was scheduled to work at Bambi's. At this point, Mary and I were speaking on the phone at least once a day, even if only for a couple of minutes. It was obvious by now that the nuns at the convent were getting more than a little annoyed and some were downright upset with my persistent calls and with Mary and me being together so much. We lost our parking spot behind Carvel's because after the policeman gave us a warning, it felt too risky.

On Saturday morning, we made a plan to meet at the school after I was finished going to the stores for my mother. Mary had a reason to go to her classroom since she was still settling in for the new school year. I had a reason to go to the school and that was to see Mary. Knowing we could only be together for about an hour, I ran as fast as I could to not miss a moment. Mary went into the building first, leaving the door open for me. I followed shortly behind. We could not risk being seen walking in together.

Mr. Smith was the school janitor; a nice polite man, he was well respected. And he always seemed to be around. The weekend seemed safe, but I did have the thought that he might be there working on a project, which made me a little nervous. But I kept going toward our meeting place, and we were finally alone. Mary was standing in front of her desk and leaning against it. I went to her immediately, and, of course, we started kissing as if we hadn't seen one another in years. While Mary was leaning against her desk, I leaned into her and because of her height, the next thing we knew, she was lying with her back on top of the desk. In my passionate state, the next thing I knew I was on top of her. Both of us were fully clothed and without any premeditation, I was doing what came naturally to a man. I was moving and just as I was reaching my moment of gratification, we both thought we heard a sound. Frightened, we scrambled to our feet, Mary putting on her eyeglasses and fixing her hair while I tried to compose myself. Looking down, she could tell I was at my height of excitement, and she put her hand over my pants. "Anthony, how does something that big go into a person?"

"Mary, I don't know. I honestly don't know."

Everybody's Talking 'Bout Us

Whatever sound we heard or thought we heard, our passionate moment was interrupted. Either way, it saved us from venturing into new physical territory, which scared both of us. After that incident, we went back to what we were doing before, which was enjoying one another's company, making out, and a little touching. I realized it really wasn't about sex, and I didn't have the need to go any further. Neither did Mary. We were content.

Still, the risks we took being in love for the first time and the physical need to be together left us resenting the time we were separated. The nights I worked at Bambi's, Mary would park around the corner waiting for me to get off, and we would go park on the side street. Of course, she did not drive me to my house; it was better that I walked home alone. The pull was so strong and the places to hide were dwindling so much so that it didn't embarrass me anymore to visit Mary at the convent. Finally, there was a positive reason to wear the Timex watch—clocking my running time to get to the convent as quickly as possible while building up my stamina and speed. Once there, I'd catch my breath before ringing the doorbell. Every other nun would answer the door except Mary. "How could this be?" I asked. "You're the only one who never answers the door."

She told me that it gave some of the other women a chance to make their unhappiness with the relationship clear. When the door opened, I would get that look of *Oh, it's you again,* before they pointed to the stairs to the basement. It also gave them a chance to point out that us being together was getting out of hand. The basement was a spacious room more like a lounge and game room with a couch and some chairs and also a ping pong table. In the beginning we would just hit the ball back and forth so that the nuns one floor above would hear us just having an innocent game of ping pong. Although, with my frequent visits, no one ever came down the stairs, the threat was still there. One night, I stayed longer than usual. We were making out leaning against a window with the shade down. When I left, feeling that the world was closing in on us, I turned around and realized if anyone had been watching from the street they could probably see our silhouette against the shade.

Already on high alert, I happened to see a lady on the sidewalk who I knew from shopping for my mother. Assuming she saw everything that had just transpired gave me a chill to my bones. To make my fear even stronger, the very next day when I went to the butcher, the same lady was there and didn't seem as friendly. Was this just in my mind? Suddenly the love I always had for Rosedale, Queens, this little hamlet that was still in the New York city limits that I called the Urban Mayberry, changed from giving me that cozy small-town feeling into a place where everyone knew everyone else's business. I didn't think that "everybody was talking at me." I thought everybody was talking about Mary and me.

I realized that what Mary and I had was filling the void left after Gramps had his second nervous breakdown. She enabled me to deal with my mother's verbal battering. Just like my gramps, Mary could always tell when hurtful words had just taken place, even though I tried my best not to show it living by the code of not airing out your dirty laundry. She would intuitively tell me, "You know you can't hide. You wear your heart on you sleeve." Amazingly, she would speak to me almost word for word the way my gramps used to speak to me, reassuring me that I was special and the most unique young man she had ever met. She said, "You're so sensitive. You know, you're an old soul."

Although I didn't know what "old soul" meant, I took it as a compliment. Her words helped to reverse the beaten-down attitude I had before meeting her. Our relationship enabled me to feel happy that I was born, happy that my mother didn't abort me, flush me down the drain, or give me up for adoption. I was feeling happy to be alive again, beginning to feel free of guilt and not caring if I ruined my mother's life. Now

I just wanted to live a life and bide my time, to bust loose from the tight rein of my mother's control. She was losing her grip. Of course, I never brought up my past to Mary. I didn't think she would understand my early experiences—my life with the Mazzines or that my first family gathering was at a prison. At the time I was ashamed of my childhood.

While my mother was losing her grip on me, the Mets were tightening their grip on first place. They were not letting up and just kept winning in wild and unusual fashion. On September 12th, they beat the Pirates in a double header; both games were won by the score of 1-0. Once again with remarkable pitching, the pitchers did not allow even one run in two games. Making it more unusual was that the only runs driven in were by the pitchers.

On September 15th, the Mets beat the Cardinals' ace pitcher, Steve Carlton. He had set a record of striking out nineteen batters, and he still lost because my favorite Met player, Ron Swoboda, hit two home runs with a man on base beating them 4-3. September 24th, it was official: Gary Gentry pitched yet another shutout for the Mets winning 6-0 as they clinched the National East title. They were going to the playoffs! That night thousands of young fans went onto the field in celebration. They tore up the turf wanting to save a piece of history. Some put a little piece of earth in their freezer, and to this day, some people say they still have it. There were security guards trying to hold back the crowds, but they were overwhelmed by the sea of humanity and let people just enjoy their moment.

That night was not emotional for me. By now, I was fully confident that the Mets were going all the way to the World Series and would win it. There seemed to be some kind of force of nature, fate, God, or whatever you believe in that took over. There was nothing for me to do but sit back and enjoy this once-in-a-lifetime event. I had a very strange feeling that it was time for me to let go of the Mets and share them with the world. The only analogy I can make is what it must feel like to have children and to let them grow up. You still love them but know it's time for them to be on their own. It was a very strange feeling to have about a baseball team. Gil Hodges and the Mets ended up winning thirty-eight of their last forty-nine games, a twenty-seven-game improvement from the year before. That year they went past the two million count of fans who came to watch the Mets play in person. The Mets were on their way to face the National Western division champions, the heavy hitting power of Hank Aaron, and the Atlanta Braves.

The Winds of Change

After the Mets clinched first place, Met fever swept across New York City. With a week to go before the playoffs, there was also change in the air sweeping across the country. Civil rights, women's rights, gay rights, and the anti-war movements were all pushing ahead. The Viet Nam war had many young men just a little older than me fighting to be allowed to vote at age eighteen since they were allowed to die for their country at eighteen. Taking all this in at the same time was dizzying and exhilarating. During that week, Mary and some other teachers went to an anti-war demonstration. When she came back, she told me she went to march for me so that when I turned eighteen, I wouldn't have to go to Viet Nam. Puzzled, I said that four years from now, surely the war would be over. Her reply was, "Don't be so sure. Four years will go by in the blink of an eye."

When you're fourteen, four years seems like a century, but it warmed my heart that she cared about me and my future. The world was changing, and it felt good to be alive and aware and in love. Change even

238

came to professional baseball. To mark their 100-year anniversary, they broke the National and the American leagues into two divisions—east and west. The winner of each league would face off in the World Series, but they had to play the best of five game playoffs first.

That week before the playoffs, when not working at Bambi's, I was running to the convent, just so that Mary and I could reminisce about all that had transpired since we had met a year earlier. One night that week, we spent the time playing "Remember When . . ." I started with "Remember how afraid I was when I first saw you? I thought you were mean."

She said, "When I first met you, I thought you were so quiet."

Then we went further:

"Remember the first games we went to when we had to take other kids with us?"

"Remember the first game we went to alone?"

"Remember our first clumsy kiss in the paper supply room?"

"Remember when the cop pulled us over after making out behind Carvel Ice Cream?"

"Remember when my mother gave us tickets to go to a Broadway opening?"

And, of course, "Remember September 8th, the greatest game ever?"

After we tired ourselves out, I kissed Mary goodnight. As I ran home, I felt that this was the first

time since Gramps was institutionalized that the wind was at my back rather than in my face.

On paper there was no way that the Atlanta Braves could match the brilliant pitching staff of the Mets, but they did have power in good hitters. Statistically, good pitching always beats good hitting. But that would be in a usual year and 1969 was not a usual year. The western division champs roughed up the young Mets pitchers. And then it happened—the Mets offense put on a hitting display of their own. Even the weakest hitters of the Mets offense came alive. A total team effort in clutch hitting enabled the Mets to come up with a different hero every game. The Mets, who hadn't scored many runs all year, outscored the Braves in three straight games, two in Atlanta and the final game in New York. Once again, the fans poured out onto the field, and I watched the celebration from home. We were on our way to the first World Series. The feeling of pride that went through my veins that day made all the days of losing worth it.

I was still getting accustomed to my new high school. I now had physical education classes and my own locker and gym outfit, which we never had in Catholic school. The week before the World Series, the coach surprised us by telling us to follow him outside. As he looked at this bunch of freshmen, he said, "I'm going to put you in groups of five and I want you to run around the track once."

He separated us by height and weight. As I looked

at the oval track, I was not intimidated at all by the task. I thought it was shorter than the run I made on a daily basis. Because I was 5'4" and skinny, I was in the first group to run. The coach, who didn't even know our names yet, tried to make it feel like an official race. We stood at the starting line; he fired the blank gun in the air, and we were off. I didn't know any of the boys who were running, but I could tell they were going much too fast. Or maybe they were trying to show off for the coach. Growing up in the Mazzine family, I had watched enough horse races to learn about pacing. Following the pack and not really exerting myself, we went around the first turn. Still staying in the back of the pack I kept my eyes on them; they still were going much too fast, and when we reached the straight away, I was still last, but full of confidence. By the time the second turn on the oval came, I could see their legs getting heavy. By now, they were running very slowly. On the final turn, I felt I'd waited long enough; it was time to make my move and I turned it on. Now, as I passed them, each kid seemed like they were standing still. With the finish line in sight, I poured it on, and I was thinking I was in the Olympics. Some of the other kids didn't even finish and others slowly came in a long time after I did. The coach asked me, "Where did you learn to run like that and pace yourself?"

I told him I'd been practicing. Of course, I couldn't tell him I ran to a convent every day.

Met Magic

Friday, the day before the World Series, I tried my best to concentrate on my classes at school, but it was futile as my mind kept drifting to the games and how they would unfold. That evening when I was working at Bambi's, Mary came in with a couple of other nuns. Although they were in civilian clothes, they were easy to spot, all wearing conservative clothing—knee-length skirts in the shade of blue or brown—and sporting similar hairstyles. They were still getting used to not wearing habits. Mary, by far, was the tallest and most broad-shouldered. She knew it drove me crazy when they came in. But, she explained, "This is where they want to come because Bambi's has the greatest selection of greeting cards."

Usually when the nuns came to Bambi's, I would turn red with embarrassment because I knew how upset they were about our relationship. I'd run and hide in the back room. But, this time, Mary stopped me before I could do that, whispering that she just wanted to see me before the big game. She also said that she would be watching and rooting from the convent.

I told her, "Please pray because you have a direct line to God, and we're going to need all the prayers we can get."

That night I could not fall asleep, but that was okay because I really didn't want to sleep. Nervous and fidgety, I was consumed with Saturday's game. Being fully aware that the 1969 Baltimore Orioles were the superior team, I was also sure my Mets would prevail. *How?* was the question I couldn't answer, but there was a feeling deep inside me that they would win. It would take a miracle, but then again I believed in miracles.

The 1969 Orioles were considered the greatest team assembled since the 1927 Yankees. Those were the days of Babe Ruth and Lou Gehrig. The whole starting lineup for the Orioles could make up an all-star team, and they had a pitching staff to match. Their manager, Earl Weaver, was the complete opposite of Gil Hodges. He was notoriously combative and argumentative; he made Leo Durocher look calm. The team he led had the likes of Frank Robinson and Brooks Robinson to name a couple. The Mets didn't have any stars other than Tom Seaver, and he was a pitcher, which meant he only played every fourth game. The Mets had relied on clutch hitting and a great young pitching staff. When the Mets won, each day produced a different hero. This was certainly a David versus Goliath situation.

Saturday, October 11th was the day I had dreamed of my whole young life. My Mighty Mouse Mets were going to play their first World Series game! I was doing what had become my routine all season long—pacing nervously in anticipation as if I was Gil Hodges. The hours waiting for the game to begin could not have passed more slowly. I still had errands to run for my mother. She and everyone on my block knew what this game meant to me, so it was a perfect opportunity for her to do her routine. She casually took her time to give me her order for the butcher. Every time I thought I was on my way out the door with her list, she stopped me in my tracks to add another item. When she saw how upset I was with her taking her time, she said one of her favorite lines, "It's just a game. So what if you miss a little?"

I ran to my room because I was positive I'd be in the butcher's shop when the game began. I took my transistor radio and then grabbed the list from her hand, and I was on the run slamming the door behind me. I couldn't get any reception on the transistor but was lucky because the butcher had the radio on just like every other business on 243rd Street. Now, it seemed, everyone was a Met fan and swore that they had always been one. Well, almost everyone. Right after the National Anthem played, a man behind the counter, a nonbeliever, told me, "Your Mets are finished now. There's no way they can beat Baltimore."

I quietly replied, "Time will tell."

Having Tom Seaver on the mound for the Mets brought me a great sense of security. He had been more than amazing all season long. But while I was still at the butcher's, in the first inning with his very first pitch, it was hit for a home run. My heart sank; the game has just begun and already we were losing. I wasn't even at home yet to watch the game. I started thinking about what the man had told me about the Mets never being able to beat Baltimore. For one moment, I thought we had met our match.

Seaver just wasn't up to par that day and the Mets never really got anything going against the Orioles ace pitcher and went on to lose the game, 4-1. After the game, I ran to a phone booth to call Mary. She was concerned about how I was handling this loss, but I surprised her with my optimism by telling her that if we could just win tomorrow, everything would be okay. We just needed to get out of Baltimore alive because the three games after that would be played at home in Shea Stadium in New York. That night, I pinned all my hopes and dreams on Jerry Koosman, the starting pitcher of the second game, the young left-hander who had also been terrific all season long.

Sunday, October 12th. Fortunately, there were no interruptions from my mother. I started my pacing in my room early. More than usual, that day was a do-or-die day. If we lost again, it would be just about over, but if we could win this one, it would be a whole new series. Finally it was game time, and I got a surprise from my father; he was going to sit and watch the game with me. Since I didn't like any distractions or questions when I was intensely into a game, his company was okay because he knew baseball inside and out; he had been taught from an early age by Grandpa Mazzine, and he had taught me about the wonderful world of baseball.

Game two was a nail biter, the kind of game I relished as I hung on to each and every pitch. I was relieved that Koosman had his stuff and Baltimore seemed limp; they couldn't get anything going, so much so, that they didn't even get a hit until the seventh inning. The Mets were able to get two runs with some timely hitting and they went on to win the game 2-1. We were alive and well, and my father said it was a great game and he was happy for me that they won. He then predicted that the Mets would win the series.

I called Mary and we were both thrilled. Monday was an off day for the teams to travel back to New York. In my mind, it was not a day off, and Tuesday could not come soon enough. The waiting was the hardest part. It was also a great feeling to be looking forward to something that has taken over your whole being.

Monday, October 13th. My father and I arrived home almost simultaneously, him from work and me from school. He was very excited about a surprise he had for me. In front of my mother, he announced that he had gotten hold of tickets for the next three games, telling us both that someone he knew owed him a favor. By that time I knew that was how the city operated. Everybody owes someone a favor, and if you had grown up in the Mazzine culture, that is baked into your being. You called the Mazzines if you had a problem, and they took care of it. On the other hand, if a Mazzine wanted something, it would be good if you came through for them. It was like an insurance policy. This pipeline ran through the neighborhood without interruption.

My father was thrilled to be able to do this for me, and I felt terrible in trying to let him down softly. I told him that I really didn't want to go to the games but needed to watch them quietly, alone, and in seclusion. I explained that the crowds interrupted my concentration and the people who attended the World Series are people who probably had never been to a game before. Many of them don't even care; they just want to be at the World Series. I also said that I took the games much more seriously than the average person. I have stayed that way my entire life. If there's a sporting event that interests me or is important to me, I'd much rather watch from home. For instance, I've never been to a Super Bowl party. (It would have been different at the time if Mary and I were able to watch it together, but that was not possible.)

At first my father seemed disappointed, maybe even a little hurt, but then my words sank in, and I saw in his face his mood turn to one of pride—pride that he had taught me so much about baseball and pride that my love for the game was so intense. He understood and let me off the hook without me feeling too much guilt. Letting me know that *he* owed someone a favor, he made a call. The man on the other end was thrilled to have the tickets and said he would take his son to the game.

My mother, on the other hand, would not drop this issue, saying, "What kind of kid doesn't want to go the World Series? Your father went to all that trouble and that's how you repay him, you ungrateful brat. You ought to be ashamed of yourself." She kept going and finally my father shushed her, which was unusual, and told her he understood my decision. But she wasn't finished. "You really stink. Let the other man enjoy the games with his son." I put my head down and didn't say a word knowing saying something would only make things worse.

After this episode, the tension was so great that I thought it best to leave for a while. I went around the corner to call Mary, making sure that I had extra change for the pay phone— this call would probably be a long one. Because I needed privacy, I had started using the phone booth in the old-fashioned luncheonette. Betty, the owner, seemed to be getting annoyed with the constant use of her phone when I wasn't buying anything. I opened the wooden doors that folded out like an accordion. I was hoping Mary would answer the phone at the convent, but of course, she didn't. I knew I was annoying the other nuns with my constant calls, but Mary was my only outlet. I told her about my father and the ticket situation and explained that maybe if it was us going together, I might feel differently. But that was impossible because these were day games and she could not get away from her nun and teacher duties to go to a baseball game, even for the World Series. I explained to her that I still felt bad thinking that I hurt my father. She responded by telling me my father was a good man, and his gesture was very thoughtful, but she fully understood the way I felt.

Mary never mentioned my mother, but she didn't have to. It was a good thing I brought extra change because it was a long conversation. We talked about the peace movement and the moratoriums taking place in Manhattan. She said she might be attending one on the coming weekend. I told her it would be great if the World Series was over by then. It was my dream to have the Mets win the next three games for the home fans. Somehow I brought the Mets and the protests against the war together in my mind; wanting peace and being a Mets fan went together. Even the Mets pitching ace, Tom Seaver, proclaimed to some sports reporters that when he took the mound on Wednesday, he would be pitching for peace. But, I told Mary, it was one game at a time and first let's win on Tuesday.

Tuesday, October 14th. The Orioles were happy not to have to face Tom Seaver or Jerry Koosman. They believed they could easily beat Gary Gentry, another young member that was starting for the Mets. But they were not thinking about the one main ingredient that the Mets had going. Magic! On that beautiful Tuesday afternoon, the magic that the Mets had all season was on full display. Gary Gentry pitched a great game, but he needed a little help from his friends, and he got it. Tommy Agee put on a show of his own with two spectacular catches, one in left center field and one in right center field. He alone saved five runs. His two great defensive plays are considered by many baseball historians as the two greatest catches in one World Series game. Gil Hodges, who had made all the right moves all year long, brought in a very young Nolan Ryan in the late innings when Gentry got into some trouble.

The hard-throwing future Hall of Famer closed the door on Baltimore. Now the Mets were ahead two games to one in the series. With Tom Seaver starting for New York the next day, we were looking good. After the game, I couldn't wait to call Mary about this thrilling win. This time I bought a candy bar when I walked into the luncheonette to appease Betty, and she smiled. She could tell I was walking a foot off the ground like almost every New Yorker.

I was in my favorite phone booth and it must have been my lucky day because this time Mary answered the phone. She knew it would be me. Of course, I went over the whole game. I could not control my excitement. We made a plan that she would be waiting for me when I got off from work at Bambi's the next night. Before I hung up, I reminded her that Tom Seaver would be pitching for peace.

Wednesday, October 15th, was exactly two months

after Woodstock. There was a spirit in the air, maybe one that only a teenager could feel when he is idealistic and believes he can change the world; nothing is out of reach and anything is possible. It's a feeling that everyone should have at least once in their lives. And for me, it didn't hurt to be in love when your team was on the way to winning the World Series against all odds. Add to this that Tom Seaver, the star on the team, told a reporter, "If the Mets can win the World Series, we should be able to end the war in Viet Nam," confirming my belief that being for peace and a Mets fan went together.

For Wednesday's game all the celebrities, dignitaries, and politicians were on hand to make an appearance to see history in the making. There was extra seating for the overflow crowd with bleachers put up behind the outfield wall. Over 57,000 people were on hand, making it the largest crowd ever at Shea Stadium. On that day, Tom Seaver was superb, and Baltimore was dazzled by his pitching. At one point, the fiery manager of the Orioles, Earl Weaver, had had enough of Met Magic and started arguing with the umpire behind home plate. He couldn't believe that he had the better team and still could not win against the Mets. When he didn't shut up, he was thrown out of the game.

For the first time in thirty-five years, a manager in a World Series game was thrown out. The rest of the game definitely would increase his frustration. In the ninth inning, when the Orioles were trying to get something going, once again, my favorite Met, Ron Swoboda, made what I consider to be the greatest diving catch in right field and saved the game, allowing Baltimore to get only one run. Because we were tied at 1-1 in the tenth inning, the Mets got a run on a very controversial call, the kind of call that always used to go against them. Met Magic was in full bloom as they won 2-1. Now we were only one game away from being the world champs.

Of course, I was over the moon when I went to work at Bambi's. When I walked in, Bambi gave me a big hug and a wet kiss on the cheek that smelled like cigarettes and beer. He was so happy for me. Mary was in the car waiting for me as I got off from work. In the car, we had one hour to talk and make out. When I gave her the last kiss goodnight, she told me that she was going to an anti-war protest the coming weekend. Everything was happening at once, and that wonderful feeling was hanging all around me.

October 16th, Thursday. It was almost a foregone conclusion that the Mets would win. With Koosman on the mound, Baltimore seemed defeated and demoralized. They tried to put up a good fight, but it was too late. Cleon Jones, the left fielder, made the final and winning play of the series. He dropped on one knee, and some fans were already on the field. It was the third time in less than a month that the whole city erupted in celebration, and the city went wild. People were beeping their horns and dancing in the streets.

They were throwing confetti out of Manhattan office windows. Everybody loved everybody—black people, white people, people who didn't know one another were hugging each other. At Shea Stadium, the old professor Casey Stengel, the original Mets Manager, went to Gil Hodges to congratulate him. Mrs. Joan Payson was adjusting her hat and crying. Then Mrs. Hodges began to cry and then everybody started crying. Pearl Bailey, who was present, was asked what she thought of the Mets, and said, "They're simply amazing."

At that moment, I was wishing my gramps were with me for this moment. The reason why Ron Swoboda was my favorite Met was because when Gramps and I watched a game, and, if Swoboda struck out, Gramps would call him "soda pop," but when he hit a home run, he knew how to pronounce Swoboda. And, on that great day, Swoboda made it even more poignant. In the locker room when all the players were drinking and spraying one another with champagne, he got up on a table and proclaimed, "We are the saints of lost causes!"

John Ianniello (Cousin John) and Tony during our wild days. Cousin John is the handsome one.

Tony with friends, Ed Kowalczyk (Big Ed), a childhood friend, and John Bencivenga (Johnny Rotten), a friend and partner in owning two delis, on one of the many nights they accompanied Tony to try out new songs in clubs in Greeenwich Village.

The Toast of the Town

Gil Hodges and the Mets did not have to fly home for their homecoming parade. Having won the World Series at Shea Stadium, they were home. Met mania flowed through the streets of New York and more ticker tape was thrown out of Manhattan office windows than on the day of the moon landing parade. The whole team also appeared on the Ed Sullivan Show. They even came out with a record album of songs with baseball themes. They sang their hearts out. Fifty years later, I still have that recording as one of my souvenirs of that year. Mary and I were flying high from the tremendous outpouring of love and enthusiasm for our team. The Mets were the toast of the town.

Mary and I, however, were not the toast of the town. We were the talk of the town. The nuns were getting increasingly aggravated by my daily calls and frequent visits to the convent. My mother was getting increasingly aggravated with the amount of time I was spending with Mary. This was even more frustrating because in the weeks and months following the Mets pulling off the impossible dream, I wanted to spend every waking moment with Mary. Being able to share my dream with someone I was in love with made it all the more satisfying.

At a time when I felt the walls closing in on us, an opportunity to spend time with her came up during Christmas vacation when schools were closed. Mary asked me if I would take a ride with her to visit her sister in Westchester County so that she could drop off Christmas gifts for her niece and nephew. Of course, I jumped at the opportunity and asked Ed to fill in at work for me. He agreed not only because he liked making the extra money, but also because I hadn't ratted him out when he was stealing from Bambi.

The day we planned to visit her sister, I left the house as if I were going to work. Mary was waiting for me in the car around the corner. I wanted to kiss her so badly, but it was broad daylight, so I had to restrain myself. She reminded me that it would be a long drive. I told her that I didn't care as long as I was with her. She thanked me, saying she needed the moral support. She said, "Whenever I see my sister, I get a knot in my stomach."

I asked why.

She turned to me and said, "Ever since we were kids, my sister had the looks and the boyfriends. Then she married a wonderful man who works on Wall Street, and now she has two great children and lives in a beautiful house in an upscale neighborhood. Yet, she finds every opportunity she gets to criticize me." She went on to say, "I want to make sure that her husband will be there when we get there. He always helps break the ice."

The ride went quickly, and we arrived at the house. I realized I had never been in a neighborhood quite like this. Just as Mary hoped, her brother-in-law had come home from work. Mary asked if I wanted to come in, and I told her I'd rather wait in the car. I said, "After hearing about your sister, I don't want to meet her, and my face is covered with acne."

From my viewpoint in the passenger seat, I could see through the picture window how attractive and feminine her sister was compared to Mary. When they greeted each other, there was a coldness about the scene. I also saw how warm and friendly her brother-in-law was to Mary. She only stayed long enough to give her niece and nephew their gifts. She came back to the car and said, "I made it. It's always difficult." She was relieved that her once-a-year visit to her sister was over.

On the way home, Mary confided to me in a way she hadn't ever before. "Anthony, in a strange way, I don't regret or resent being a nun, but I do feel like I never had a choice. Because I wasn't pretty like my sister, I was groomed from high school not to think about marriage. I was strongly encouraged, even pushed, to pursue a religious life and enter the convent right after senior year. Having you in my life and feeling your love for me and our love for each other has made me wonder for the first time what my life would have been like if I'd hadn't been pushed into joining the convent. Maybe there was another path for me to take where I met someone and had a family." She added, "You know, the same way your mother tries to control and mold you into what she wants you to be, my family pushed me into doing something they wanted for me, not something I chose for myself. I now resent the message that my only option in life was to be a nun." She sighed and leaned back in her seat. I was touched by what she had revealed to me and also felt slightly uneasy. I didn't dwell on it then, and we enjoyed the rest of the ride home, talking and listening to music like we always had.

When I babysat for my sister, I'd use the opportunity to call Mary without having to run to the phone booth. One winter night when I was babysitting, our telephone routine came to a crashing end. When my parents arrived home my mother was fuming. She told me she'd been trying to call me for two hours and kept getting a busy signal; this was before call-waiting and caller ID. I was totally caught off guard. She let me have it, asking if I was on phone with that "goddam nun" again. I put my head down and went to my room as she kept yelling about "the nun." The world seemed to be closing in on me, but I would not let it dampen my happiness or the relationship I had with Mary. I also never made the mistake of using the home phone again.

By then, the safest way to see Mary was actually at the convent. I had gotten over being embarrassed anymore, and I didn't care which sour-faced nun opened the door for me. I wasn't willing to let anything or anyone get in our way. It was the price I had to pay to hold her in my arms and enjoy the fresh, clean scent of lemon in her auburn hair. Once in her arms I felt that God had given me the gift of another guardian angel. Surprisingly, at first I didn't like the wrapping the gift had come in, but once opened, I realized that I had found a person who in loving me, gave me self-assurance and confidence. When I arrived at the convent, I would be shown to the basement and, as time went on, we didn't even pretend to play ping pong anymore.

Music always came through for me, and Mama Cass did it again with a song called, "You Have to Make Your Own Kind of Music" emphasizing the line, "Even if no one else will sing along." That said it all for us. In November, Harry Nilsson came out with the song, "I Guess the Lord Must Live in New York City," supporting my theory that there was divine intervention in the Mets winning. As the months rolled along, so did Mary and me. I thought I had a master plan for us to bring in the new year.

On New Year's Eve, my parents or their friends would celebrate by throwing a big party in one of their homes. This year, I was delighted that the party would not be at our house. I would be babysitting that night. My plan was to invite Mary to come over and celebrate—just the two of us. I thought it would be a great way to recap this amazing year we had shared. It was only a little over a year since she had stunned me with that surprising Christmas gift, the Snoopy Friendship book. Within the year that I'd known and fallen in love with Mary, men had landed on the moon, we saw Woodstock, we sang songs of peace together, and after that glorious September 8th baseball game, my amazing Mets got to walk in the sun. On that New Year's Eve, we wouldn't have to get on the phone; it seemed so safe for us to be together. What could go wrong?

As I anxiously waited for my parents to leave and for Mary to arrive, suddenly everything changed. The phone rang, and my father picked up. I could hear in his voice that something was terribly wrong. He was very shook up and saddened by the time he got off the phone. He told my mother that the father of the man hosting the party had died suddenly of a massive heart attack. Of course, now Mary and I would not be with each other, after all.

Hearing this terrible news, I dashed out of the house and ran like I was Jesse Owens to the phone booth in Betty's Luncheonette. I was a wreck. I had to reach Mary before she left the convent. Thank God, she was still there. To add to the strangeness of this night, while I was explaining to her what happened, the man in the phone booth next to me collapsed from a drug overdose, and I was then surrounded by police and paramedics. At first, I could not get around the crowd and leave. I didn't want to seem insensitive to what was going, but I had to get out. Finally, I squeezed myself through a very narrow path to the door and ran home as quickly as I could. When I got back, of course my parents were sad about the news of their friend's father. Luckily, neither one of them asked questions about why I had run out of the house. As quietly as I could, I went to my room and listened to music playing softly.

When I woke up, it was 1970.

Close to You

The spirit of 1969 followed me into the new year. And so did my acne-covered face. It was worse by the day and was getting so bad that it was painful for me just to talk to someone. The only time I felt comfortable was in Mary's arms. It was still remarkable to me that she would kiss me. I felt only someone who loved me so much would be able to do that. She said it didn't bother her, but it was starting to control my life. Of course, every kid thinks they have the worst case ever. But I felt like I was the ugliest person in the world. Some adults could tell how much this was affecting me, and while some kids were calling me 'pimple face' and 'pimps' for short, I did get support and advice from very surprising people.

One day, my Spanish teacher, Mrs. Greeves, stopped me as I was leaving her class and asked me to wait until the other kids left. I thought she was going to talk to me about how low my grades were, but instead, she said, referring to my face, that she had grown children and she remembered what they had gone through. She suggested that every night when I went to sleep to use a fresh pillowcase. That simple act of kindness has stayed with me all these years. It made feel so good that someone I hardly knew cared. Bambi used humor to show he cared and said, "Anthony, all you have to do is get laid and all the pimples will go away."

But, in the end it was my father who came through. He took me to a dermatologist and listened; he bought all the medications the doctor suggested. He would take me there regularly and, at home, would take me down to the basement in the boiler room. There, he would have me sit under a sun lamp he bought for me an hour a day as he put clean hot medicated face towels on me. The smell was horrible, but it meant so much to me that I was willing to do anything. As he was doing this daily, my mother would be upstairs yelling that the smell was like rotten eggs going through the whole house and when would it end? My father quietly would say, "Don't listen to her. Let's just do what the doctor told us."

Little by little it was starting to get better, and I was starting to come out of my shell just in time to celebrate the first Earth Day with Mary in April. During that time, my music teacher played a song by Pete Seeger about pollution. He was surprised that not only did I know the song, but I was also aware of how much effort Seeger was putting into the cleaning of the Hudson River. I also told him three other songs that were about ecology, and he was impressed by how much I knew. One day, the same music teacher played a song that I had never heard. It had no lyrics, but

I found it stunning. It was called, "Variations of the Theme." It was the first time since West Side Story that I appreciated music without words. I was even more surprised when he told us that the band Blood, Sweat and Tears was playing it. To this day when I listen to that song, it puts me in a peaceful and reflective mood.

While I was focused on my face and Mary, my parents were focused on finding us a house in a new neighborhood. It all made sense. My little sister couldn't live in their room in a crib indefinitely, so we needed a house with an extra room. Also, my father was hearing terrible stories about the racial tension in my high school. Some of his friends had children who had gotten into serious fights. I never had any problems. Here, I give credit to growing up in the Mazzine culture, which enabled me to intuitively know how to handle difficult situations. They planned to move in the summer as soon as the school year was out. All I really cared about was how this was going to affect my relationship with Mary. Although I could sense subtle changes, the one I didn't notice was right in front of me.

I was still visiting the convent and calling Mary on a regular basis, and I noticed that, when we were together, she would often mention how many nuns were leaving religious life. At first I didn't think this had anything to do with me and her, but each time we spoke, she gave me little hints telling me stories of how the dating scene was going for nuns who had left the convent. Once she told me she went to a party with some ex-nuns, and a man named Tom showed an interest in her. I was glad we were on the phone so that she could not see how terribly upset I was by this news. Making matters worse, she told me her renewal of vows for continuing to be a nun were coming up soon. This happened every seven years in her religious order.

During this time, a fashion fad had become popular. Women were wearing see-through blouses to make a statement of liberation. She and some other nuns came into Bambi's for greeting cards, and I noticed that the blouse Mary was wearing allowed one to see the outline of her bra through the paisley design. As I was getting the feeling I was losing her, I made a desperate move and told her I didn't want her to wear that see-through blouse anymore. It was a demand that only an immature fifteen-year-old would make. She said, "Anthony, it is not a see-through blouse, and I'll wear the blouse if I want to."

By now in my mind, everything depended on whether or not she would renew her vows. I wanted to put her in a cocoon and not let her out in the real world, so that my world would stay safe. Ironically enough, it was the fact that the nuns no longer wore habits that made our relationship possible but was now the reason that it might end. I would have felt safer had she been in a habit, but if that were the case, we never would have happened.

My parents found a house in Valley Stream just one town over, but it was a world away. They took me for a ride to see the house and showed me the school I would be attending in September. They showed me around enthusiastically, but my mind was clearly elsewhere. I was quiet. The move was planned for late June 1970.

There were a few things I had to do before we moved. First, I went down the street to Brookville Park where there was a man-made lake. I took a run around the lake at the fastest speed I could and, when I completed the circle, I took the Timex and threw it in the lake. As I watched the water cover over it as it sank, I told myself I would never let anyone control me again. I have never worn a watch since. Second, I went to the back of the garage where, long ago, Miriam and I had buried a bottle with a note in it. I wanted to take one long last look so the imprint of that spot would be in my mind forever. It's still a dream of mine to go back to that spot and dig up the bottle. Last, but not least, since I had no friends left to say goodbye to, I went to see Bambi. We had become so close; I had been working there since I was 12. He thanked me for working for him and taking care of his dogs and told me that he knew how much I loved Tracy. Before he started to cry, he gave me another hug and wet kiss. I thanked him for all that he had taught me, and, as I was turning to leave, he said, "Remember what I told you, Anthony.

Don't worry about your pimples. They'll go away as soon as you get laid."

We settled into our new house. My room was upstairs, and this was great. I would be able to get away from any chaos going on downstairs. We had a big, beautiful backyard, and the houses were not too close together, giving us a little space. So, in my mind, if my parents were fighting, I figured the neighbors could not hear them. But, for me, the most important thing was Mary and me. I'm sure the nuns in the convent were relieved and thrilled that I wouldn't be visiting anymore. Now I would have to call Mary from the house phone. I made sure each call was short and to the point, like, "When can we get together?"

Of course, we could not see one another as often as I would have liked, but she would pick me up at the house about once a week. Sometimes, she would even stop in to say hello to my parents, which made me feel uncomfortable. But it was worth it to see Mary.

After about a month, Mary arranged for another overnight visit to Sag Harbor with some other kids. This time, my cousin John came with us. Since she arranged this, I had a feeling of safety and security that she would renew her vows and not leave the convent; we were still doing things the way we always had. When we arrived at the retreat house, it was as beautiful as I remembered. Once again while Mary was in a bathing suit sitting out on the pier with the other kids, I took my post in my favorite chair looking out the big picture window. The hit song at the time was "Close to You" by the Carpenters. As I listened to the words ". . . they long to be close to you," I realized no one wanted to be close to Mary more than I did. When Mary and the kids came in, she called me her "little old man" just like the summer before. I felt sure that she wouldn't leave the convent and we would be together like always. I was wrong.

Soon after that trip, Mary said we had to have a talk. A couple of days later she picked me up and we parked behind a different Carvel Ice Cream store. She told me that, after giving the situation of renewing her vows much thought and because of our relationship, she decided that she could no longer be a nun. She said it was time to let me go. She said I had taught her so much about herself and because of that, she had decided to leave the religious life, and it was not fair to me to take any more of my teenage years away. She said, "I'm not letting you go because I don't love you. I'm letting you go because I do love you. You have a chance to start fresh in a new neighborhood in a new school, and you need to meet kids your own age. Before you know it, you will be dating girls. You have your whole life ahead of you." I just sat in the passenger seat devastated and quiet, and she said, "I hope someday you will look back at the time we had together in a positive light."

There was a place deep inside of me that knew she was right, but I did not want to let go or lose her. In my fifteen-year-old mind, I didn't see why we couldn't just go on until I was eighteen, and we would be free. Her plans were set in motion. She told me she had already found a job as a teacher in Westchester County and would begin in the new school year. We never even got an ice cream. I just wanted to go home. When we got in front of my house, she said, "We must always remain friends."

I didn't kiss her. I just got out of the car and said goodbye. She looked so sad and pained. It looked like true sorrow. I went into the house and straight up the stairs to my room and turned on the radio, and, as if on cue, Buffy St. Marie was singing, "Stay until it's time for you to go." I felt like the words, the music, and Buffy St. Marie's voice were cradling my emotions. It was a song that Mary and I both loved and now it was becoming all too real. For about a week, I just stayed quiet, mostly in my room. One day Mary called and said she wanted to stop by to say goodbye to me and my parents before she left to start her new life. She said she would be over in about fifteen minutes. It was the longest fifteen minutes of my life. When she did arrive, my parents were very welcoming and thanked her for all the things she had done for me. She told them it was her pleasure. I just stood there and took it all in as if I didn't care. I was indifferent. I walked her to the car, and, with my parents, I had to be polite even though I didn't feel like being polite. As the car pulled away, I went back into the house and my parents said, "That was so nice of her to stop by and say goodbye before she left." They said, "She must really care about you, Anthony." I went up to my room and sat on my bed quiet, devastated, and angry.

A Kid With No Past

After Mary drove away, I was lost in a pit of despair. Gramps wasn't around, the Mets had achieved my dream, and now Mary was gone. Emotionally spent, I couldn't figure out how my little world had collapsed so fast. Just the year before, I was at the pinnacle of joy. Within days of Mary leaving, letters started arriving at my house. I was eager to get them and took some immature satisfaction knowing that she was having a difficult time adjusting to her new life and that she had found that students in the public schools showed no respect for their teachers. In each letter, she asked me to please call her—she gave me her new address and phone number to call or write. She explained that we should always remain friends, but I was in no mood to be friends. I wanted her to hurt the way I was hurting. I wanted her to realize that she made the wrong decision leaving the convent and leaving me. The letters came for months, sometimes pleading with me to get in touch with her. She ended each of the letters saying, "You'll understand some day, and, in time, your life will get better."

Mary's letters were written in code making them not too personal in case they were intercepted by my mother. They were mostly generic in content. She even sent postcards once in a while saying hello and wish you could be here. I must say that my mother never did open a letter. In my room, I hung the banners of the Mets winning the League Championship and the World Series. I put up the portraits of every Met player from the 1969 team. Looking at them, I would relive the miracle year, but at the time, I didn't even have the oomph to listen to music.

While I did read Mary's letters over and over again, I hid them in the bottom of a drawer and covered them with clothes. I never once thought of writing her back or calling her. Having all the emotions of a first broken heart, I was sad, alone, lost, and angry, and I wanted to remain angry. Somehow it gave me a false sense of control. Looking back, of course, I had no control. That's why I didn't want to play music; I was afraid that I'd burst out crying. Each day, I went through the motions to resemble some kind of normalcy.

My parents were focused on their new house and neighborhood and setting up the new room for my baby sister, which was fine with me. I just wanted to be left alone. Now that we lived in suburbia, the stores were no longer right up the street, so it fell on my father to take my mother shopping since she had never gotten her driver's license. The only positive thing I could see since Mary left was that I no longer had to endure the humiliation of buying feminine napkins.

I still wanted to hold onto my anger, but then one evening in my room watching a black and white television in my darkest hour, a video came on with a young lady singing a song called, "Beautiful People." This was long before MTV. I had never heard a voice like hers before. It was so honest and real; she sang about being alone and feelings of loneliness and longing for something to belong to. Her name was Melanie. It came to me that this was the same young lady who sang "Candles in the Rain" about her experience at Woodstock. As I listened to her quivering voice the hair on my arms stood up just like they had during that game on September 8th, 1969. I felt like she was the missing link in my life. Not long after that, a friend and I went to an old theater in Manhattan to see Melanie perform in person. She would start off the songs lightly and in the end, give them everything she had leaving me spellbound. From the opening notes, and as part of that audience, I knew I was home. Finally, I had found that feeling of belonging I was looking for. I felt like she was singing to all the lost people, giving us hope. Dylan and other songwriters opened my mind, but Melanie opened my heart.

I have been blessed. Life always seems to send a lifeline during the roughest of times. Melanie's impact was immediate and immense. Soon I started taking guitar lessons. I just wanted to get a nylon-string guitar like she played, learn some chords and to finger pick like she did. Now that I had found my tribe, I was willing to let down the icy barrier I had put up. Suddenly and unexpectedly, I was happy to be in a new neighborhood, a new school, and meeting new friends my own age. Rather than feeling lost, I was using the time to start with a clean slate—the kid without a past. Of course, I never talked about the projects, the Mazzine culture, my mother's cruelty, or Gramps's mental breakdown. Most importantly, never about Mary.

Mary's letters kept coming but less frequently, still pleading for me to get in touch with her. But I was moving on now. At that point, all I could think about was writing songs of my own. I wanted to let go of all I had been holding in. I found a way to express myself through music, and I was determined to do it.

I was now attending the same school as my cousin John. There were four years difference in our ages, but he was very mature. He was the first audience for my new songs. He was honest and supportive and would tell me what he thought of them. While the songs were flowing out of me at a rapid pace, I still could not share the secret of Mary even though most of the songs were written for her.

Another intriguing surprise came up. My parents learned of a program where they would get paid for housing my gramps because it was less expensive for the state, and he was nonviolent. He moved into the small room next to mine. We were together again. We lived like two bachelors up there, since my mother was too lazy to come up the steps. He never was the same as in our glory days but being with him on a daily basis was great for both of us.

By eleventh grade, my hair was growing longer, and I was becoming my own person. Me and my guitar, which I carried wherever I went, led me to make many friends. By this time, letters from Mary had long ago stopped. I guessed that she had given up the chance we could remain friends. Inwardly, I knew how much she had helped me and my self-confidence and dealing with my mother. Because of Mary, I was past feeling any guilt about my mother.

The length of my hair and my attire did not make my father happy—I walked around like a flower child wearing overalls and moccasins, and most of the time without a shirt—but that was not unusual for that era between fathers and sons. However, he could not be prouder of my work ethic because I had a lawn-cutting service and was also working for two dog breeders who happened to be neighbors. I even got to show dogs at Madison Square Gardens and won many ribbons along the way.

When the possibility of me being drafted and going to Viet Nam was becoming more of a reality because of my age, my father shocked me by telling me that if I got drafted and didn't want to go, he had arranged with someone he knew to get me to Canada.

I was stunned. I didn't even say thank you, but because of his reassurance, I felt I'd be protected and would not have to go to Viet Nam. I never registered for the draft. My father was a quiet man, but in retrospect, I see and appreciate how he intervened at very important moments throughout my life. After I graduated from high school, I had to pass the Selective Service Building to go to work every day, and I would look up at it and quietly thank my father.

With cousin John being my little music manager, giving me support and critiquing my new songs, I was getting more compliments each day. I am grateful that John had the foresight to record my songs in his basement and put them on two CDs. He still claims some of the songs are good, even though I cringe.

During these years, the surprises kept coming. Unexpectedly, one day my old friend, Ed, showed up at my house in his brand-new VW bug. We picked up our friendship where we left off years earlier when we were working at Bambi's, and we were back into politics, music, and coin collecting. Things were happening at a rapid pace. I couldn't believe how quickly my life was coming together. Mary had predicted that it would all be okay, and that I would meet kids my own age and have a normal teenage life. At the time, I didn't think that was possible, but it was coming true. And I was enjoying my life!

A less enjoyable occurrence happened in my senior year of high school when I mentioned to my mother that many of my friends were going to a community college and asked her if she thought I should go. I shouldn't have been surprised when I heard her say, "You know you're too dumb to go to college. Why don't you just get a job like your father? Are you too good for work?" I never brought up the topic again.

On my eighteenth birthday, I remember clearly walking toward my house and seeing my father come out of the front door. He said, "Anthony, you have a phone call."

I asked who it was. He said, "I think it's your old teacher, you know, the nun."

I ran into the house and it was Mary wishing me a happy eighteenth birthday and asking if I was ready to be friends. Excitedly, I said, "Yes, I am."

She was happy with my reply. We made a plan to have our reunion as soon as school was out. A couple of months later, I borrowed my Uncle Funzi's 1962 Pontiac and drove up to visit Mary in Bronxville, New York. She was waiting for me outside her apartment building. She looked the same to me, but when I stepped out of the car holding my guitar with my long hair and no more acne, she exclaimed, "Oh Anthony, how did you come to look like Jesus Christ?"

I said, "I had a good teacher."

We hugged and went inside. We talked and drank vodka and orange juice until the wee hours of the morning. Strangely, we did not reminisce; we just caught up on what we had been doing in the years since we hadn't seen one another. She told me about the man she was dating. She asked if I had plans to go to college. I did not have the heart to tell her what my mother had said. She would have been furious, and I didn't want to spoil our reunion. I just told her that I had not decided. She said, "You must go."

We talked and drank so much that we decided it would be best if I slept over. I slept on the couch where I belonged, and she brought me a pillow and a blanket. As she was walking away to go to her bedroom, I used some humor asking if she could at least tuck me in. She laughed and said, "Oh, you're still a little old man!"

The next morning I played her some songs that I'd written specifically for her, and she was surprised at my new-found talent and very touched. She asked, "Where did you get all this confidence?"

I replied, "I owe it all to you."

Soon after, it was time for me to go. We promised one another that we would never lose touch again, and we would be friends forever. She said, "Anthony, there's one thing I'd like to tell you before you leave. I want to apologize for what happened. I was the adult, and I should not have let it go that far. I should have known better."

She was relieved when I said, "Mary, the time we had together will always be close to my heart, and I will always cherish the memories."

It's now fifty years later, and I still cherish that time of my life.

These are the lyrics to the song I played to her on that visit.

I Hope You Feel the Way I Do
You brought the sunshine into my life
You came when it was dark and cloudy
You made me feel like I was special
And you calmed me down when I got rowdy

You saw me go through the changes
The changes that life brings
And I know we had our disagreements
But we're together so it seems

That I love you,
I hope you feel the way I do
Yes, I love you
I hope all our dreams come true

282

Melanie at the height of her fame. Her words and music opened up Tony's heart and gave him a sense of belonging.

Melanie and Tony at their reunion in 2017, reminiscing about her glory days.

Sister Margaret, a teacher at St. Pius Elementary School, and Tony at their unexpected reunion after 25 years.

284

When ITony first met Pat. There's nothing like new love.

Pat and Tony at the beach in Port Jefferson.

Epilogue

A few years after our last meeting described in the book, I attended Mary's wedding. It was an elegant affair, and I was so happy to see her happy. Her dreams had come true. She was married at the Westchester County Country Club to a kind, professional man who commuted to Manhattan for work. They bought a house in Westchester. Her life was like her sister's but without the kids. During her wedding day, I remember feeling that our relationship had played a significant part in her new life. Like we promised, Mary and I have kept in touch to this day.

Gramps lived with us for a while. He was never the same, but I am so grateful to have had him by my side during my childhood. He passed away in April 1978. I always found it interesting that I came to him in April, and he left in April. And it was baseball season. You can read a humorous story about him *A Leg to Stand On* in the chapter, "Gramps."

I grew to deeply appreciate my father Pete in his final years when we grew much closer. Regrettably, he died soon after retiring. He would be glad to know that when certain traits appear in me, my wife reminds me that I am a Mazzine. It's in the blood.

My mother, the hypochondriac, who told everyone that she's been dying since the Kennedy assassination, is alive and well and living in New York city. Sadly, her sister Jeanette, my aunt, passed away from breast cancer in her early thirties leaving her husband Funzi with five boys. When Jeanette became ill, she and my mother were not speaking to each other, and my mother had a lot of ground to make up. They reconciled, but it was bittersweet.

It was during Jeanette's illness that her oldest son, John Ianniello (Cousin John), started spending more time at our house. He and I became more like brothers than cousins and have remained close all these years. He is one of the most talented human beings I have ever met.

My poor sister took even more verbal abuse than I did and still seeks my mother's love, which she just doesn't get. But she always keeps trying. I forgive my mother for what she did to me but have more trouble forgiving her for what she did to Maria.

Amazingly, my mother gave birth to another child twenty years younger than I—my brother Peter. Somehow Peter managed to escape my mother's verbal onslaught, and, surprisingly, he was even pampered. Although he lives in Florida, we are in touch on a regular basis. He, too, has the Mazzine genes even though he never met them. I point that out when we talk, and we are both fascinated by the similarities.

By 1973, Melanie had become famous, and on February 3rd of that year, Cousin John and I pulled off a feat that could only happen to true believers. We went to Carnegie Hall without tickets on the evening Melanie recorded her birthday album. The highlight of the evening was that she personally escorted us in through the stage door, and we enjoyed the evening of a lifetime. Every February 3rd, Cousin John and I call one another to reminisce. Melanie and I had a lovely reunion in 2017 when she came to California to perform, and I reminded her of the Carnegie Hall incident. That night when she was performing, she invited me on stage to tell the tale. You can read the whole story in my book, *A Leg to Stand On*, in the chapter, "On Stage with Melanie."

One of the Mazzine brothers had a son who married the daughter of the New York crime boss, John Gotti.

Ed and I remained lifelong friends. But, of course, I never told him about Mary. She was his teacher too. An interesting coincidence happened one day in our twenties when we were driving in a part of Queens that we were not familiar with. At the same moment, we both noticed a store sign saying, "Bambi's Stationery," and at the same time said, "There's only one Bambi!" We walked in, and there was Al Bambus having a cigarette and a Rheingold Beer behind the counter just like in the old days. Bambi was delighted to see us together, and I asked him how he ended up in that location. He told me that we were too young to understand at the time, but he always opened a store, built it up, sold it, and moved to another site.

As for me, I've had many wonderful adventures and some amazing coincidences. Decades after I had left New York for a new life in California, I had been working at a restaurant, and two of my favorite guests, Mary Kay and Robert King, came in with two of their friends who happened to be nuns. One of the sisters had been working in Zimbabwe as a missionary for many years. We chatted a bit and were shocked to come to the realization that she had been one of my teachers at St. Pius, Sister Margaret. She also happened to be one of the more disapproving nuns of my relationship with Mary. However, although she was not happy with me in 1969, she seemed genuinely pleased to re-meet me. The full story is in my book, *A Leg to Stand On*, in the chapter, "A Very Special Guest."

I also had a few bumps in the road. In 2003, I was in a car accident, which led to me losing a leg, coincidentally, just as my gramps had. Later, I went through a difficult couple of years (2010-2011), but on New Year's Day of 2012, a little dog with a missing leg named Brie, owned by Don and Lois Mayo, came into my life and changed everything.

Other Books by Tony Albano

Life is a Bumpy Road: Smoothed Out by the People—and the Dogs—You Meet along the Way

A Leg to Stand On: More Stories of the People and Dogs that Keep Me Going

All Tony's books can be ordered from:

- BarnesandNoble.com, Indiebound.org, Amazon.com
- You may also purchase them at Whittakers of Carmel, Kris Kringle of Carmel, and Diggidy Dog, all on Ocean Avenue in Carmel, California

And you may even meet Tony walking with his three-legged companion, Brie.

To contact Tony, you may visit his Facebook Page, *Tony Albano, Storyteller and Author,* or his website, tonyalbanostoryteller.com. You may also email him at Tonyalbano1969@gmail.com.

To contact Nina Solomita, the editor of this book, email her at ninasolomita@gmail.com, website: ninasolomita.com.

Made in the USA
Columbia, SC
31 May 2021